Learning and Teaching with Information and Communications Technology

Series editors: Tony Adams and Sue Brindley

The role of ICT in the curriculum is much more than simply a passing trend. It provides a real opportunity for teachers of all phases and subjects to rethink fundamental pedagogical issues alongside the approaches to learning that pupils need to apply in classrooms. In this way it foregrounds the ways in which teachers can match in school the opportunities for learning provided in home and community. The series is firmly rooted in practice and also explores the theoretical underpinning of the ways in which curriculum content and skills can be developed by the effective integration of ICT in schooling. It addresses the educational needs of the early years, the primary phase and secondary subject areas. The books are appropriate for pre-service teacher training and continuing professional development as well as for those pursuing higher degrees in education.

Published and forthcoming titles:

R. Barton (ed.): *Learning and Teaching Science with ICT*
M. Hayes (ed.): *ICT in the Early Years*
A. Loveless and B. Dore (eds): *ICT in the Primary School*
M. Monteith (ed.): *Teaching Primary Literacy with ICT*

ICT IN THE PRIMARY SCHOOL

Edited by

Avril Loveless and **Babs Dore**

Open University Press
Buckingham · Philadelphia

Open University Press
Celtic Court
22 Ballmoor
Buckingham
MK18 1XW

email: enquiries@openup.co.uk
world wide web: www.openup.co.uk

and

325 Chestnut Street
Philadelphia, PA 19106, USA

First Published 2002

A catalogue record of this book is available from the British Library

ISBN   0 335 20916 5 pbk   0 335 20917 3 hbk

Library of Congress Cataloging-in-Publication Data
ICT in the primary school / edited by Avril Loveless and Babs Dore.
        p. cm. — (Learning and teaching with ICT)
        Includes bibliographical references and index.
        ISBN 0-335-20916-5 (pbk.) — ISBN 0-335-20917-3 (hard)
        1. Educational technology. 2. Information technology. 3. Computer-
assisted instruction. 4. Education, Elementary. I. Loveless, Avril. II. Dore,
Babs, 1952– III. Series.

LB1028.3 .I315 2002
372.133'4—dc21
                                                                    2002024625

Typeset by Graphicraft Limited, Hong Kong
Printed in Great Britain by Biddles Limited, Guildford and Kings Lynn

CONTENTS

LIST OF CONTRIBUTORS

Tracy Atherton is an advisory teacher for ICT, based at Highwire, the Hackney City Learning Centre in London, England. She has been a primary teacher in London for many years, taking part in a number of ICT innovations. She is a member of 'Creating Spaces', a network of independent professionals promoting creative uses of technology.

Andy Carvin is Senior Associate at the Benton Foundation's Communications Policy Program in Washington, DC. One of the coordinators of the Digital Divide Network (www.DigitalDivideNetwork.org), Andy has written numerous articles on the use of technology in communities and education, including his award-winning website, 'EdWeb: Exploring Technology and School Reform' (www.edweb.gsn.org).

Elizabeth Coppard is a primary school teacher who undertook her PGCE teacher education at the University of Brighton.

Hannah Davies was ICT projects coordinator at the Centre for Language in Primary Education (CLPE) in London, England, where she helped to establish their NOF ICT training. She now works at Highwire, the Hackney City Learning Centre, and coordinates Creating Spaces, a network of independent professionals promoting creative uses of technology.

Babs Dore is a senior lecturer at the University of Brighton where she lectures on ICT in primary education. She was a primary school teacher for 12 years and had a particular interest in science education. Her current research interests are in supporting student learning through the appropriate use of ICT.

Toni Downes is Associate Professor and Head of the School of Education and Early Childhood Studies in the College of Arts, Education and Social Sciences at the University of Western Sydney, Australia. She has been involved in a number of research initiatives, including children's use of new technologies in the home. She is also the secretary of the Working Group 3.5 on Informatics and Elementary Education for the International Federation of Information Processors (IFIP).

David Hicks is a faculty member in social studies education in the Curry School of Education at the University of Virginia, USA. The Curry School has played a primary role in devising teaching tools that effectively tap the latest advances in computing and telecommunications, adopting a collaborative approach and assembling teams of experts that transcend departmental boundaries and disciplines.

Heikki Kynäslahti is a researcher in the Department of Teacher Education at Helsinki University, Finland.

Avril Loveless is Principal Lecturer in ICT in Education at the University of Brighton. She has published a number of books and papers relating to the use of ICT in learning and teaching. Her current research interests include pedagogy and ICT and the creative use of digital technologies, particularly in the visual arts. She has been the chair of the Association for Information Technology in Teacher Education (ITTE) and is a member of Creating Spaces.

Cheryl L. Mason is a faculty member in social studies education in the Curry School of Education at the University of Virginia, USA.

Olivia O'Sullivan is based at the CLPE where she has designed and presented a range of innovative courses and materials for teachers.

Aarno Rönkä works as an English lecturer in the Secondary Teacher Training School at the University of Helsinki.

Janne Sariola is project manager in the Educational Centre for ICT at the University of Helsinki.

Seppo Tella used to be Professor of Media Education at the University of Helsinki Media Education Centre. At present he is Professor of Foreign Language Education at the Department of Teacher Education.

Martin Torjussen is a primary school teacher in Brighton, England. He was a PGCE student at the University of Brighton, following broad experience in the commercial sector and teaching overseas. His interests include the creative use of new technologies to support and extend children's learning.

Nicola Yelland is Professor and Head of the Department of School and Early Childhood at the RMIT University in Melbourne, Australia. Her research interests centre on the use of ICT by teachers and children in a variety of contexts. Nicola teaches undergraduate and graduate classes in mathematics education and ICT, and works with teachers in professional development activities.

SERIES EDITORS'
PREFACE

Perhaps the heart of this volume is best encapsulated in the fundamental question that Loveless poses at the end of her initial chapter: 'What are schools *for* in a Knowledge Society?'

In answering this challenging question, the various contributors draw upon some long-standing traditions in primary education. Primary teaching is associated with child-centred learning where the acquisition of performance and thinking skills provides the context for professional thinking in practice. Primary practitioners *think* across subjects as well as *teach* across subjects. ICT is itself an integratory factor and, within the primary perspective, we are seeing more innovation using ICT in the classroom in the teaching and learning process than is often evident elsewhere. From the earliest days of the introduction of computers in schools, much of the software developed was for the primary curriculum, at first to teach well established topics in new ways, but later to teach new things made possible only through the new technologies.

The present volume continues the tradition of primary innovation. Although individual chapters necessarily deal with discrete elements of the curriculum, the volume as a whole represents a commonality of ways of thinking which permeates the chapters. Establishing practical and intellectual links between the chapters, and a common thread of thinking across them, constitutes an essential element in the book's construction and in this way itself reflects the practice of the good primary classroom, a point explored by Loveless in her opening chapter. A characteristic feature is that the authors have frequently addressed *why* we are teaching with ICT in particular ways as well as *how* the teaching is to be done.

The volume therefore offers shared ways of thinking about ICT – a conceptual framework which both challenges established ways of working and demonstrates, with a focus on higher order thinking, pedagogies which go beyond the immediate needs of the classroom.

Primary teachers of the twenty-first century are working with pupils by whom ICT is seen as 'normal'. They are the generation who are growing up with ICT as a non-remarkable feature of their world, in the same way as an earlier generation took television for granted. When the pupils of the present day generation arrive at school, the use of ICT in the classroom can become an extension of a pre-school experience many of them will have had in the home. Within the context of the expectations of both pupils and parents, primary teachers are almost inevitably presented with the demand to work with the new technologies and as such are developing appropriate classrooms approaches.

This is not being achieved without considerable need for both personal and professional development. The Primary sector has had access to some strong support in this respect through the work of Primary Professional Associations (for example MAPE). ICT also brings with it opportunities beyond the conventional media for professional development, with computer mediated conferencing, as described in Dore's chapter. It is interesting, moreover, to see how the boundaries between novice and expert are broken down through ICT, as evidenced in work of the PGCE trainees described in the final chapter. This chapter also raises questions about assessment and ICT and to what extent tasks involving this medium can ever be said to be 'finished'. The potential for constantly revisiting the task is unlimited.

The authors suggest that the potential of ICT to enable children to show and create knowledge lies in their teachers' critical understanding of the deeper purposes of learning and the ways in which learners, teachers and new technologies can interact with each other.

So in seeking to construct an answer to 'What are schools for in a Knowledge Society?' the authors ask themselves and their readers three fundamental questions:

- What does ICT offer to the quality of young children's learning?
- What are some of the key issues which teachers need to address concerning the Information Society?
- How does children's experience of ICT in school relate to their learning experiences beyond the classroom?

These questions provide a mapping of the concerns for this stage of schooling, to be explored through the reflective practice of the primary classroom. It is through the discussions evident in this volume that the answers begin to become apparent and direct the attention of all of us to the challenges to schooling presented by the Information Society.

Anthony Adams and Sue Brindley

INTRODUCTION

Avril Loveless and
Babs Dore

ICT (information and communication technology) *in the primary school* is a topic of fast-developing discussion, policy and practice in many countries. Governments have prioritized the allocation of resources to making ICT accessible to students and staff in schools, providing opportunities for training teachers and outlining the forms of ICT in the curriculum as a resource to support learning – as a subject in its own right and as a catalyst for higher-order thinking processes. Teachers in primary classrooms have dealt with significant changes in their use of ICT in recent years. They have developed their own personal and professional applications and adapted their teaching strategies for different learning environments, such as an ICT suite, portable computers in class, home-school links and virtual 'spaces' for communication between learners and colleagues.

Changes in practice take time to plan, try out, evaluate and adapt. The use of ICT in primary schools is developing within a community of teachers, pupils, friends, families, peers and members of the wider and various communities that schools serve. In such an area, 'experts' and 'novices' are not easily defined by traditional roles and all members of the community can contribute their experience from a number of spheres to an unfolding and shared understanding of the questions 'What?' and 'Why?' when we use ICT in primary school settings. At the time of writing this book, many primary teachers are engaged in examining their reasons for using ICT in their work with young children. They are considering a range of challenging questions in their profession. How do they manage a range of models of access to ICT resources? How do they plan appropriate learning experiences for children? How do they assess their children's achievements? How do these achievements relate to children's immediate learning experiences? How do they relate to more long-term goals for participating in a democratic and critically informed society?

Accompanying these initiatives in schools are many guidelines, books, handbooks, training courses, discussion groups and exhibitions to support teachers and student teachers. The authors of this book were invited to contribute chapters that would not only share examples of practices for working with ICT in the classroom, but also provoke a critical approach for ideas and innovation. They present a range of perspectives on the issues, drawing upon their experience and expertise in the different countries and spheres in which they work. Each of the authors works closely with ICT with young children and teacher colleagues – as classroom practitioners, as teacher educators, as researchers, as advisers to policy makers. Each has a commitment to the quality of children's learning and a critical approach to the use of new technologies for their own sake. They challenge us to think carefully about how ICT might be used in primary schools, not just to follow current statutory curriculum and assessment requirements. They ask questions about the contribution ICT can make to children's representing what they know and can do. They also share their vision of the ways in which ICT can play a powerful role in creating learning environments in which children can explore, construct, test and refine their knowledge.

The book is structured to reflect the development of a 'conversation' about ICT in the primary school, although each of the chapters can also stand alone. The first four chapters present discussions about the priorities and purposes for using ICT with young children from the perspectives of work, research and policy in the UK, Australia, the USA and Finland. The next four chapters focus upon rich environments for children to engage in key processes: finding things out, communicating and exchanging information, developing ideas and making things happen. The emphasis is on the richness of the learning environment for children, not necessarily the sophistication of the technologies employed! The final two chapters address the central issues of professional preparation and development.

The book was conceived and written with a particular audience in mind: the teachers, teacher educators and student teachers with whom we work and with whom we have had opportunities to discuss not only 'how' to use ICT, but also 'why' it might be worth thinking about and developing in the primary classroom.

ICT IN THE PRIMARY CURRICULUM

Avril Loveless

The first chapter begins by asking questions about the nature of young children's experiences and expectations with information and communication technology (ICT) and the mismatch, perceived by many of them, between their experiences at home, their experiences at school and the understanding of their parents, carers and teachers. These issues are related to descriptions of the 'information age' or 'knowledge society', the demands of preparing people to participate in such a society and the links with current understandings of learning. It is then suggested that there are characteristics of ICT which make a distinctive contribution to the kinds of higher-order, critical, creative and collaborative thinking that underpins the requirements of the knowledge society. It will also be argued that, despite a current focus on the use of ICT to raise standards in literacy and numeracy, as recognized in national, standardized tests, the National Curriculum for ICT in England provides a useful framework for 'ICT capability' or 'information literacy'. Such capability enables children to demonstrate the development of their knowledge, understanding and skill in making 'informed judgements about when and where to use ICT to best effect, and to consider its implications for home and work both now and in the future' (DfEE 1999: 96).

Introduction

In the last year of the twentieth century, a teacher in an English primary school was asked why she thought she should bother to use ICT in her teaching. Her reply was short: 'Because it's out there!' Before hurrying off to do her playground duty, she described her perceptions of how ICT was having an impact on her own life and the lives of the children in a variety of situations – from online shopping to text messages on mobile phones, from entertainment to the world of work. She felt a responsibility not only to 'equip' her children to deal with the ways in which ICT gave them access to information, but also to support them in making choices about the ways in which they used ICT in critical and creative ways. She was also concerned, however, that the opportunities she had to develop this approach in the children's school experience were currently constrained by a number of factors: her own confidence and competence in using fast-changing technologies; the access to ICT resources within her school at times and in spaces which were useful; the requirements of the curriculum and assessment frameworks in which she worked; and the expectations of the children whose experience of using ICT beyond the school challenged her as she tried to plan and prepare her teaching. She was aware of the significant social and cultural impact of ICT in the world in which she and her children lived, and welcomed the initiatives in education which raised the profile of ICT in the context of teaching and learning. She was also aware of the tensions that exist between the practical demands of a busy classroom and the potential of ICT to challenge the time, space and pace of authentic learning environments which might support learners in the twenty-first century. Indeed, she was very conscious of the word 'potential', feeling that despite the promise of ICT there was little evidence that it was having much immediate impact on her classroom work and that she and her colleagues in school would need to take a long-term, reflective view of the reasons why they thought they should be using ICT in a primary school.

All commentaries on the use of ICT in education face the issue of the fast-changing nature of the forms of the technologies themselves and the impact they have in different situations. During the last five years there has been a noticeable shift in student teachers' levels of confidence, competence and attitudes to using ICT in their professional development, and many practising teachers have undertaken training and widened their experience of using ICT in their professional work. Yet the underlying issues of how ICT might support learning in the curriculum and the development of higher-order, complex thinking must still be discussed. These issues can be shared, challenged and evaluated in order to develop our understanding of how our education in schools addresses children's needs, achievements and potential within learning communities. The chapters in this book present a number of perspectives on these different experiences in classroom practice, in school contexts and in the cultures of different countries. This first chapter sets the scene by focusing on some of the issues which primary teachers at the beginning of the twenty-first century are considering in their own preparation, planning and professional development in relation to the role that ICT could play.

A mismatch between home and school?

Jack Sanger describes the mismatch between children and young people's experience of digital technologies in their social and cultural lives and in school classrooms as a 'cultural airlock', and calls for a radical reappraisal of the structures of schooling to meet the needs of individual learners (Sanger 2001). The slow pace of adoption, appropriation and change in relation to technology in schools has been contrasted with that in the wider economic and social sphere. Government initiatives to raise the profile of ICT in education, provide access to ICT resources and support training for teachers have had some impact on classrooms and school experiences, but time-travelling teachers from the nineteenth century may well recognize little change in contemporary classrooms from their own models of teaching (Papert 1993). Teachers' resistance to technological change in classroom practices has been noted from the introduction of wireless to the arrival of computers (Cuban 1986), and the predictions that the educational system will be revolutionized by ICT have not come to pass (Selwyn 1999). Indeed, the report by the Office for Standards in Education (Ofsted) on *ICT in Schools* indicates that while effective use of ICT in teaching subjects across the curriculum is increasing, good practice remains uncommon (Ofsted 2001).

How well informed are we of the ways in which children and young people make sense of ICT and appropriate it for their own purposes? Research conducted for the British Library and British Film Institute to investigate young people's engagement with screen technologies highlighted the range of experiences with TV, videos, computer games and personal computers. Many of these experiences were, however, unmediated by parents, carers or teachers who did not appear able to demonstrate their own experience of popular culture in sharing and discussing the children's responses to, and interpretations of, their activities, whether they be 'shoot 'em up' games or information and images from websites. Some adults expressed concern about the nature of children's use of videos and computers, but were unaware of the ways in which children were engaging with, and making sense of, their experiences, whether as solitary individuals or in social and collaborative groups (Sanger *et al.* 1997). Other researchers highlight the gap between children's preferred use of computers in the home and their restricted or 'boring' use at school, while proposing that home use is not a simple and uniform phenomenon,

but has the potential for a variety of appropriations, uses and constructions that are not always reflected in school experiences (Downes 1997;
Sutherland *et al.* 2000).

The ScreenPlay project in the UK explored the ways in which children
and young people, aged 9–11 and 12–15 engaged with screen technologies outside school, and identified a number of issues relating to the
nature and quality of their experiences. Access to screen technologies
was fast-changing, as more families upgraded their facilities and renego-
tiated the 'family rules' for who could do what, when and with whom in
the family or network of friends. Children noted that those with easy
and frequent access, well supported within their families, often seemed
to have preferential access at school because of their increased competence with ICT. An interesting finding of the research related to the
nature of the learning experiences with screen technologies in the home:
contrary to a popular myth of 'cyberkids' with inherent and spontaneous computer capabilities, the children reported that they exploited a
range of strategies for learning, mostly from playful discovery and asking
friends and family, but occasionally from online help or manuals. The
activities in which they became involved were often quite narrow in
focus, but substantial in depth, relating closely to their personal interests
and enthusiasms. They contrasted this model, where their learning was
incidental within a context of their own choosing, with their experiences
at school where the teacher chose and directed the activity, the learning
itself was the focus and there was often insufficient time to explore the
resources and ideas behind the activity (Sutherland *et al.* 2000).

Recognizing that many studies of children's use of ICT focus on those
children who have sufficient access and interest to use it at all, the
project also identified children who were 'low users' and the analysis of
surveys and interviews with these children proposed that the notion of
cyberkids is problematic. The children gave a range of reasons for their
attitudes to, and degrees of use of, ICT, from socioeconomic purchasing
priorities within their families to a perceived lack of relevance of computers to their own interests and perceptions of themselves as 'cool', not
'geeks' and 'having a life' (Facer and Furlong 2000).

The situation of children's access and attitudes to ICT is fast-moving
and teachers need to be aware of the changes in the social and cultural
contexts in which children engage with new technologies. At the time of
writing a large-scale, national research project is being undertaken in the
UK. The aim of the Impact2 Project is to assess the impact of networked
technologies on educational attainment in English schools, asking key
questions: 'Is learning with ICT more of the same or can ICT transform
learning?' and 'Why are young people such rapid learners of and with
ICT?' Early baseline data from the project indicates that there were
interesting aspects to the two areas of access to, and representations of,
network technologies. First, access to a range of ICT in the home, such

as games consoles, computers, the Internet, email addresses and personal mobile phones was high. In the group of 730 10-year-old children surveyed, over 75 per cent had a computer at home, over 50 per cent had an email address and nearly 20 per cent had a personal mobile phone. Second, when asked to draw diagrams about 'Computers in My World', the children drew a range of images which represented the complexity of their understanding of the links and connections between the different elements of technologies – such as computers, mobile phones and games consoles – and their functions – from sending text messages to robot control in factories and communicating with satellites (Somekh 2001). Acknowledging the complexity and sophistication of the children's engagement with technologies in their wider communities is an important aspect of the teacher's role. Peter Scrimshaw described the need for the 'networked teacher' to be involved in a 'deeper appraisal of the teacher's role than is commonly recognised, requiring a fundamental and continual process of rethinking what is taught, how it is taught, and why' (Scrimshaw 1997: 112).

Despite the complex and problematic nature of children's varied experience of ICT in school and home settings, ICT in education is often promoted by the suppliers of hardware and software as a 'solution' to problems in learning and teaching. An analysis of advertisements for ICT resources, aimed at teachers as the audience, highlights the presentation of educational ICT as enabling the 'dream' of individualized learning for children, contrasting with the 'nightmare' of teacher confusion and misunderstanding of the new technologies. Images of ICT as solutions to both futuristic and traditional views of teaching and schooling are projected without critical appraisal of the roles of, and interactions between, the teachers and the children (Dawes and Selwyn 1999). Buckingham and his colleagues investigated the marketing discourse in promoting educational technology to teachers and parents. They identified the changing relationship between 'education' and 'entertainment' in the promotion of resources in two situations: at the BETT Show, an annual exhibition of educational ICT resources in London, and in specialist magazines and catalogues for parents wishing to know more about educational ICT for their children. Their work also identified recurring themes of 'empowerment', 'emancipation' and 'solutions' running alongside messages of 'good' parents and teachers dealing with the dangers of Internet access for their children. 'Edutainment' was promoted as bringing fun into learning in order to help children do better in their school work and assessments (Buckingham *et al.* 2001). Such commercial promotions of 'solutions' do little to highlight the learning processes in which children engage with ICT, nor to explore how these might be extended in the classroom beyond the need to raise achievements in traditional assessments. Stephen Heppell (1994) used an analogy to illustrate the absurdity of providing new tools and media for children to express and demonstrate their learning while testing traditional outcomes. He described the scenario in which we provide new, high-performance motor cars and test the impact on the nation's capability by putting the drivers on to horses and examining their dressage skills!

The world in which young children are engaging with and developing their use of ICT is complex, moving quickly and challenging to the purposes of the current curriculum and assessment frameworks. To adopt the simplistic view that teaching and learning with ICT is a solution to yesterday's problems would be an abdication of responsibility to the children in our society. Teachers need to be able to make informed and imaginative decisions about how the curriculum and the teaching strategies which children encounter in schools enable them to become critical and creative participants in a 'knowledge age', not passive consumers of 'information'.

The knowledge age

Some have claimed that Year 1 of the knowledge age happened in the USA in 1991 when spending for information technology (IT), such as telecommunications and computers, exceeded spending for industrial-age capital such as engines, machinery and industrial equipment (Stewart 1997 cited in Trilling and Hood 1999). Such a shift from industrial manufacturing processes to the making, manipulation and moving of information also echoes a shift in the purposes and values which underpin work in such a society. These are in turn echoed in the values which underpin education systems and expectations within that society.

In exploring the questions relating to the purpose and relevance of schools and teachers in a knowledge age, some have considered the demands of the workplace and the links with the requirements of the education system. The schooling systems of the nineteenth century reflected the need for a literate and numerate workforce in the factories and counting houses of the industrial society: how will the schooling systems of the twenty-first century reflect the needs of people in the knowledge age on a global scale?

Others, however, challenge the role of education as the means to meet the needs of the corporate economy, and view its purpose as being to promote democracy and participation in societies which recognize the impact of their actions and interactions and the importance of equality, diversity and cooperation in human fulfilment. Trilling and Hood (1999) have identified, albeit in a somewhat contrived manner relying heavily on alliteration, a categorization of the Seven Cs – skills for the knowledge age:

- *critical thinking and doing* – problem-solving, research, analysis, project management;

- *creativity* – new knowledge creation, best-fit design solutions, artful storytelling;
- *collaboration* – cooperation, compromise, consensus, community-building;
- *cross-cultural understanding* – engagement across diverse ethnic, language, cultural, knowledge and organizational structures;
- *communication* – exchanging and sharing information, using media appropriately and effectively;
- *computing* – appropriate and effective use of electronic information and communications technologies;
- *career and learning self-reliance* – managing change, lifelong learning and career redefinition.

Such a framework can also be shown to be reflected in current understandings of models of the variety of ways in which people learn. Using another set of Cs, Trilling and Hood argue that there is a match between learning theory and knowledge skills, raising an interesting, and unresolved, question as to whether our models of learning are created to express our social and cultural needs in different times. They present a range of models of learning which provide different perspectives on the ways in which we learn for a variety of purposes:

- *Context* – drawing on the work of people such as Lave and Wenger (1991), learning is situated in environments and contexts which can provide relevance and richness to the depth of the learning experience.
- *Construction* – drawing on the influences of Piaget, constructivism views knowledge as constructed through action and interaction, assimilation, accommodation and adaptation in the 'concrete' and 'symbolic' worlds. Constructionism, as described for example by Papert (1993), develops these ideas and relates them to the role of the designing and building of artefacts or models which assist in the development of mental models of the world.
- *Caring* – drawing on a wide range of work in the affective domain, this aspects of learning is demonstrated in the positive impact of intrinsic motivation and reliance, persistence and commitment to problem-solving (Covington 1998).
- *Competence* – understandings of the nature of 'intelligence' have broadened to recognize the ways in which it is exhibited in a variety of behaviours and contexts, acknowledging multiple learning approaches and expressions (Gardner 1993).
- *Community* – the social and cultural contexts of learning are seen as powerful influences, as people learn from and with each other in 'communities of practice', recognizing the contexts of knowledge, power, teaching, learning and structure within those communities (Wenger 1998).

Such an analysis of the requirements of the knowledge society highlights how the characteristics and qualities of knowledge skills can be developed through the different approaches to learning, focusing on people being active and valued members of learning communities. If we accept that we are part of the development of, and debate about, our society in a knowledge age, and recognize the centrality of continuing participation and engagement with learning, then we need to address questions about the nature and purposes of our schools and the people who play roles within them. In his book, *The Control of Education*, John Tomlinson wrote about the importance of teachers' understanding of the history of education; how this shapes the material with which they work every day; and how democratic ideas can be fostered or constrained: 'This is not to suggest that anyone has thought that education was the only or even the most important influence on the next generation, but because the kind of schooling we decide to offer our young is the clearest public statement we can make about the kind of society we want *them* to build' (Tomlinson 1993: 62).

How then do we acknowledge the centrality of higher-order, complex thinking skills in our schools? How do we evaluate and analyse the school curriculum that children experience in terms of these critical, creative and collaborative approaches to learning? How do our teaching strategies provide opportunities for children to demonstrate, evaluate and develop these complex thinking processes in the work that they do and the knowledge, skills and understanding that they learn and use in their lives outside school? How do we help children to learn how to learn?

Why ICT?

In a society in which ICT has a significant social, cultural and economic impact, how might it play a role in developing complex thinking for members of our society? What is ICT good at, and how does it make a distinctive contribution to teaching and learning activities? What makes ICT motivating to use in a variety of contexts? What are the characteristics of ICT which can be exploited in order for it to make a contribution as a resource, as a tool and as a catalyst for new ways of working in the curriculum? This section will argue that there are particular features of ICT which can support authentic learning and that the National Curriculum for ICT in the UK provides a framework in which the processes of higher-order, complex thinking can be supported in the context of dealing with information in useful and effective ways. ICT capability is therefore related to a much deeper understanding of information and knowledge, and is not just a facility with a range techniques and skills with particular technologies and software applications.

Distinctive features of ICT

There are features of ICT which can help us to analyse how it might make a contribution to teaching and learning processes which is distinctive from other media, tools or resources. The features are: *interactivity, provisionality, capacity, range* and *speed*, and when these are recognized and engaged in activities which use ICT, the experience is more authentic.

Interactivity can engage users at a number of levels, from the playing of an adventure game on a games console to the monitoring of space probes in international space programmes. These two different activities have in common the ways in which ICT can give immediate and dynamic feedback and response to decisions and actions made by the user. Children could play an adventure game, undertake a search of the world wide web, display a graph of the changes detected by temperature sensors over a period of time or create and navigate a hypermedia presentation. Using ICT in each of these activities enables children to make decisions, see the consequences and act upon the feedback accordingly. Having curiosity and confidence to engage in such interactions might not be easy or comfortable for some children or adults, so encouraging children to explore, to learn from dead ends and frustrations and to develop perseverance in trying out ideas and learning from feedback is an important aspect of the teacher's interaction in these processes.

The *provisionality* of ICT enables users to make changes, try out alternatives and keep a 'trace' of the development of ideas. This feature can be recognized immediately in the writing of text with a word processor, which enables the writer to make changes at a number of levels. Early versions can be saved for comparison, or returned to for further development. Visual images can be modified and manipulated from the initial image created or captured on the screen, and saved along the way as ideas change and develop. As with interactivity, teachers can promote positive attitudes to working with and exploiting the provisionality of ICT. They can model, discuss and make explicit the processes of evaluation, changing ideas and reviewing work and encourage children to see the advantages of crafting and revisiting ideas in the light of feedback from 'critical friends' or after time for reflection.

ICT demonstrates *capacity* and *range* in the ways in which teachers and children can gain access to vast amounts of information in the form of text, visual images and sound. This information might be accessed on a CD-ROM available in the classroom, on a website located on the other side of the world or by discussion with people living and working in a different time zone and geographical place. Gaining access to such a range of information does not, however, ensure that there is understanding of the authority and authenticity of that information. Teachers play an important role in supporting children's critical approach to searching for and evaluating information, as well as providing them with strategies to understand how to exploit the capacity and range of the technologies.

The *speed* and automatic functions of ICT allow tasks of storing, changing and displaying information to be carried out by the technology, enabling users to read, observe, interrogate, interpret, analyse and synthesize information at higher levels. Many routine activities such as capturing and organizing data, monitoring change, checking spellings and grammar, carrying out calculations, drawing graphs and presenting findings can be done using ICT, leaving the children time to ask questions and think about the meaning of the information with which they are presented. Teachers play a role in supporting the children in developing their understanding of the processes involved and the contribution that ICT can make in providing a range of representations of information as a starting point for critical and creative thinking.

A framework for ICT capability

UK policy for the development of ICT in education is informed by four perspectives which themselves relate to particular purposes for the use of ICT as a resource:

- to promote vocational goals in preparing pupils for future work;
- to raise standards in pupils' achievement;
- to increase teacher effectiveness and efficiency in professional preparation and presentation;
- to support, promote and extend learning.

It is this last perspective, the use of ICT to support, promote and extend learning in its broadest sense, which is the focus of the chapters in this book. *ICT capability* is a term which is used to describe the knowledge, skills and understanding which contribute to a range of processes in which we use ICT to deal with information in meaningful, effective and appropriate ways. Definitions of *ICT capability* in appropriate and purposeful contexts for learning have developed within UK government policy since the publication of *Information Technology from 5 to 16*, which presented a clear view of the role of IT in enriching and extending learning in ways which require learners to be active, evaluative and critical in their use of the technologies (DES 1989). The 1990 version of the National Curriculum for IT included the notion of skill, but still highlights the importance of knowledge and understanding in a changing field which presents new opportunities. The 1995 definition of IT capability in the National Curriculum presented a view which emphasizes the purpose and variety of contexts in which individuals actively use technologies to 'analyse, process and present information and to model, measure and control external events' (DfE 1995). The definition of ICT capability presented in the National Curriculum 2000 is a broad view of capability for pupils in the wider context of their learning:

> ICT prepares pupils to participate in a rapidly changing world in which work and other activities are increasingly transformed by access to varied and developing technology. Pupils use ICT to find, explore, analyse, exchange and present information responsibly, creatively with discrimination. They learn how to employ ICT to enable rapid access to ideas and experiences from a wide range of people, communities and cultures. Increased capability in the use of ICT promotes initiative and independent learning, with pupils being able to make informed judgements about when and where to use ICT to best effect and to consider its implications for home and work, both now and in the future.
>
> (DfEE 1999: 99)

These definitions encompass perspectives of ICT capability as a higher-order cerebral activity and a potential for action, as well as a possession of skill or techniques with particular applications or ICT resources. They also include a view of capability as being embedded in a purposeful context for the individual.

The National Curriculum for England identifies the 'programmes of study' and 'attainment targets' from which schools can develop their planning and organization of the curriculum. The programmes of study identify the matters, skills and processes of a curriculum subject which pupils should be taught. The attainment targets describe the expected standards of pupils' performance and progression within the subject throughout the key stages. The framework for the knowledge, skills and understanding in the ICT curriculum is presented in four aspects:

- finding things out;
- developing ideas and making things happen;
- exchanging and sharing information;
- reviewing, modifying and evaluating work as it progresses.

These aspects reflect the ways in which people work with ICT for particular purposes. They focus on the reasons for using ICT, not on a list of specific applications, software or resources. The knowledge, skills and understanding encompassed in these four aspects are taught in a broader context (or breadth of study) of working with a range of information, exploring a variety of ICT tools, working with others and investigating and comparing the different uses of ICT inside and outside school. It can be useful to think of these aspects as 'strands' which are distinctive, but can weave around each other in building ICT capability. The details of the programmes of study for Key Stages 1 and 2 for pupils aged 5–7 and 7–11 are given below:

Finding things out
Pupils should be taught:

- *Key Stage 1*
  How to gather information from a variety of sources
  How to enter and store information in a variety of forms
  How to retrieve information that has been stored
- *Key Stage 2*
  To talk about what information they need and how they can find and use it
  How to prepare information for development using ICT, including selecting suitable sources, finding information, classifying it and checking it for accuracy

Developing ideas and making things happen
Pupils should be taught:

- *Key Stage 1*
  To use text, tables, images and sound to develop their ideas
  How to select from and add to information they have retrieved for particular purposes
  To try things out and explore what happens in real and imaginary situations
- *Key Stage 2*
  How to develop and refine ideas by bringing together, organizing and reorganizing text, tables, images and sound as appropriate
  How to create, test, improve and refine sequences of instructions to make things happen and to monitor events and respond to them
  To use simulations and explore models in order to answer 'What would happen if . . . ?' questions, to investigate and evaluate the effect of changing values and to identify patterns and relationships

Exchanging and sharing information
Pupils should be taught:

- *Key Stage 1*
  How to share their ideas by presenting information in a variety of forms
  To present their completed work effectively
- *Key Stage 2*
  How to share and exchange information in a variety of forms, including email
  To be sensitive to the needs of the audience and think carefully about the content and quality when communicating information

Reviewing, modifying and evaluating work as it progresses
Pupils should be taught:

- *Key Stage 1*
  To review what they have done to help them develop their ideas
  To describe the effects of their actions
  To talk about what they might change in future work
- *Key Stage 2*
  To review what they and others have done to help them develop their ideas
  To describe and talk about the effectiveness of their work with ICT, comparing it with other methods and considering the effect it has on others
  To talk about how they could improve further work

Breadth of study
Pupils should be taught the knowledge, skills and understanding through:

- *Key Stage 1*
  Working with a range of information to investigate the different ways it can be presented
  Exploring a variety of ICT tools
  Talking about the uses of ICT inside and outside school
- *Key Stage 2*
  Working with a range of information to consider its characteristics and purposes
  Working with others to explore a variety of information sources and ICT tools
  Investigating and comparing the uses of ICT inside and outside school

ICT capability can be seen to be demonstrated in the active engagement of techniques and skills with a range of technologies within purposeful contexts which require degrees of choice, control and critical understanding.

It is in the attainment target for assessing children's 'levels' of ICT capability that the progression within the processes of complex thinking in these elements can be discerned. In the National Curriculum in England, the attainment targets indicate the progression that children can make within curriculum subjects and 'levels' are assigned in formative and summative teacher assessments and national Standard Assessment Tests (SATs). In Key Stage 1 the range of levels within which the great majority of pupils are expected to work is between 1 and 3, with the majority attaining Level 2 at age 7 at the end of the key stage. In Key Stage 2 the range of levels for the great majority of pupils is 2 to 5, with the majority attaining Level 4 at age 11.

The levels in the attainment target, although crudely applied as 'best-fit' descriptions of children's achievements, indicate the nature of the progression which can be made in the different processes of ICT capability.

These processes develop from the children being aware of and able to describe the ways in which they can work with ICT, to an understanding of purpose, audience and the need for accuracy and validity in dealing with information. In *'Finding things out'*, for example, children can demonstrate early awareness by exploring information from various sources and showing that they know it exists in different forms (Level 1). They can make progress in developing these processes in order to demonstrate that they can select the information they need for different purposes, check its accuracy and organize it in a form suitable for processing (Level 5). Similarly, in *'Developing ideas and making things happen'*, young children can demonstrate this process at Level 2 when they plan and give instructions to make things happen and use ICT to explore what happens in real and imaginary situations. At Level 5 they demonstrate that they can create sequences of instructions to control events, and understand the need to be precise when framing and sequencing instructions.

ICT capability, as described in the National Curriculum, therefore draws upon and promotes the 'knowledge skills' of communication, critical thinking, creativity, collaboration, cross-cultural understanding and the use of ICT resources. It can be fostered and expressed in a variety of learning contexts which reflect competence, construction, caring and community.

ICT and complex thinking

The National Curriculum for ICT in England is a framework for considering ICT capability and its relationship to higher order and complex thinking processes. It is useful to consider the ways in which the common ICT resources and applications used in the primary classroom can be seen to provide support for this way of working and thinking, rather than just acquiring sets of skills and techniques for operating the applications themselves. This discussion is placed within the context of the variety of ways in which children gain access to communication technologies in school and in the home, and the demands that this makes upon developing appropriate teaching strategies and expectations. The way in which ICT itself plays a role in supporting teachers' professional development in these areas is discussed in Chapter 9.

In recent years, many primary schools have developed models of access to ICT resources within the classroom and school environments. Computers can be grouped in 'clusters' in classrooms or resource areas, in dedicated computer suites or in sets of portable units such as laptops or palmtops. Many schools also have shared resources such as digital cameras and scanners for capturing visual images, sensors for data logging, programmable 'robot' toys and electronic whiteboards for whole-class interaction with applications. These different models of access call for different teaching strategies and clarity in planning the purpose of the children's experiences. Dedicated suites are helpful in providing opportunities for whole-class demonstration, teaching and practice of techniques and skills with a wide range of applications. The teacher is able to make the focus of the lesson very clear and the children can be given time to explore and learn through discovery and collaboration within the curriculum context of the activity. There are limitations to this model in that timetables and the booking of the suite can often militate against the children being able to take their time to become familiar with software in order to use it in an authentic way to support their curriculum activity. Teachers working in schools which have set up ICT suites also recognize the ideal of having access to ICT resources in a more flexible way back in the classroom or resource area, to enable children to use the technologies when they are appropriate within the activity. The portability and flexibility of laptop computers for staff and pupils has been shown to be a positive element in supporting change in the integration of ICT in teaching and learning (BECTA 1998; Loveless *et al.* 2000). Drawing upon expectations of children's access to ICT outside school is an area which needs further research and attention. Schools could make positive use of the range of ways in which children use ICT in the home. There is, however, the important issue of our understanding of equity and quality of access, which is discussed in more detail in Chapter 3.

The argument in this chapter has been that young children's experience of using ICT in their primary schools takes place in the wider context of the social, cultural, economic and political arena of education, raising questions about how school experience might relate to home and leisure experience, and how school expectations might relate to society's expectations of the purposes of schooling. The framework of the National Curriculum for ICT provides an expectation of progression in using ICT to support *processes*, such as finding things out, developing ideas and making things happen, exchanging and sharing information and reviewing, modifying and evaluating. The features of ICT which contribute to these processes have also been considered in the ways in which provisionality, interactivity, capacity, range and speed enable the representation of knowledge. How do these broad-brush ideas relate to the practical reality of the range of ICT resources and software applications which can be found in many primary schools? How might primary teachers approach the planning and preparation of the use of ICT in the curriculum which reflects the aim of promoting ICT capability and higher-order, complex thinking?

'Computers as mindtools'

In Chapter 10, Martin Torjussen discusses the different levels at which teachers need to plan for experiences which address children's learning in the curriculum, in ICT capability and in ICT skills and techniques. Woven through these three elements is the underlying purpose of the nature and quality of the children's thinking as they engage in activities and processes. David Jonassen has outlined a useful framework for 'thinking about thinking' with ICTs in which he describes his approach to *'computers as mindtools'*. He argues that computers are not tools to 'teach' children, in the sense of 'tell and assess their recall of what they were told', but intellectual tools to help children to assemble, construct and represent their knowledge in a variety of ways (Jonassen 2000: 3). His classification of the common types of software applications used in schools can map quite closely to the 'strands' of ICT capability described in the ICT National Curriculum, and provides a way of thinking about those applications in a context related to critical, creative and collaborative thinking.

Jonassen's framework describes these 'mindtools' as *semantic organization tools*, *dynamic modelling tools*, *interpretation tools*, *knowledge construction tools* and *conversation tools*. *Communication tools* can also be added to this framework.

Semantic organization tools are those applications, such as databases and concept maps, which enable learners to identify questions and the nature of the data required to explore possible answers. These tools play a role in the way in which children can form and test hypotheses, collect, organize, store and interrogate information, develop searching and sorting strategies to retrieve information, develop evaluation criteria for the accuracy and validity of the information, analyse the representation of the information and identify both answers to problems and new questions. Such tools are therefore useful in developing ICT capability in terms of finding things out, developing ideas and making things happen, exchanging and sharing information, and reviewing, modifying and evaluating information.

Dynamic modelling tools are applications such as spreadsheets, microworlds (e.g. Logo), simulations and adventure games which enable learners to ask the question, 'What would happen if . . . ?' and see the causes and consequences of actions and decisions in the patterns, representations and relationships that develop. Exploring causal links with such tools provides opportunities for open-ended, conjectural enquiry, generating and testing hypotheses, generalizing rules from experiences and representing knowledge in multiple ways: from charts derived from data in spreadsheets to dynamic visualizations displayed in data logging or simulations. The main focus of ICT capability with these tools is developing ideas and making things happen, and reviewing, modifying and evaluating information.

Interpretation tools are applications which enable learners to collect and interpret information that relates to their enquiries arising from their initial curiosities and questions. The world wide web, multimedia information provided on CD-ROMs and Internet search engines are examples of the ways in which information can be organized and presented in order to facilitate navigation, browsing and the making of connections between a variety of sources of information. Such hypermedia applications, which have hypertext links between different elements of the information, enable the learner to articulate their enquiry and navigate their way through sources in order to identify salient information. To use these facilities effectively, learners need to develop information retrieval strategies, from choosing key words, phrases and questions to critically evaluating the authenticity and validity of the information they find. A key to effective use of hypermedia and the world wide web is *intentionality*, through which learners identify the goal and focus of their enquiry and develop ICT capability in finding things out, developing ideas and making things happen, and reviewing, modifying and evaluating information. Chapter 5 addresses many of these issues of dealing with rich information.

Knowledge construction tools also draw on hypermedia authoring applications which allow hypertext links for navigation through material in a non-linear manner. The focus of these tools, however, is on the opportunities for the learner to create the connections between information and present these in multiple ways, often using multimedia text, images and sound. The effective use of such tools requires a broad ICT capability including the purpose of the presentation, planning and review, researching, organizing and linking information and an understanding of the ways in which multimedia and interactivity can engage and involve an audience in sharing the knowledge. Chapter 8 focuses on the use of multimedia in knowledge construction and communication.

Conversation tools include applications such as email, file transfer, bulletin boards, discussion forums and videoconferencing, which enable learners to communicate directly with others, either immediately and at the same time (synchronously) or at different times (asynchronously). The use of these tools requires users to orientate themselves in relation to the environment and other participating groups, establish roles, seek and share information, negotiate understandings and decisions, and reflect upon and construct responses to others. Chapter 9 develops the discussion of how teachers can use these tools to support their own professional development and reflective practice, and Chapter 4 demonstrates how children can engage with these technologies.

Jonassen's framework does not include the significant range of applications which also support exchanging and sharing information for learners, which can be described as *communication tools*. These include word processors, desktop publishers, graphics packages and multimedia presentation applications which enable users to compose, outline, redraft, edit and present information in multiple forms appropriately for different purposes and audiences, supporting ICT capability in developing ideas and making things happen, and exchanging and sharing information. Loveless and Taylor (2000) presented their work with these tools in the visual arts and Hannah Davies and Olivia O'Sullivan discuss these areas in relation to literacy in Chapter 7.

Complex thinking which reflects critical, creative and collaborative dimensions does not happen in a vacuum and the use of a range of ICT is not neutral. The values and beliefs which underpin teachers' professional knowledge are reflected in the ways in which they conduct their interactions with the children and their colleagues, and the nature of the learning environments which they establish in their classrooms. Authentic learning takes place in contexts which are meaningful and relevant to learners, enabling them to make connections between different aspects of their thinking, their feelings and their experiences. Michael Bonnett (1997) discussed his concerns about the issues related to the use of computers in schools by stressing the importance of the interaction of teachers and learners in the context in which the child's understanding is developing. Teachers and peers are able to acknowledge and respond to the quality of children's previous experiences, and they can provide responses, questions and explanations which require the learner to puzzle, reflect and discuss instead of receive the 'correct' answer. Complex thinking can be stimulated and challenged by the use of ICT, but not *defined* by it, and the ways in which it is used in the primary classroom reflect the teachers' understanding of the distinctive contribution it can make to the wider contexts of learning.

ICT in the primary school

The authors of the chapters in this book each present a view of the potential of ICT to support young children's learning, both in curriculum subject areas and in their capacities to develop higher-order, critical and creative thinking. The sheer presence of the technology itself in the classroom can often be very daunting, cluttering up both physical space with cables and connections, and mental space in planning for access to equipment and familiarization with skills and techniques. Teachers have high expectations placed upon them in preparing learning experiences to develop learners' knowledge and understanding in the curriculum, in their ICT capability, in their ICT skills and in their thinking processes. It is however important to be mindful of the wider social, cultural and economic contexts in which children engage with ICT and to reflect on how these relate to practices in primary schools in order to address the deeper question: 'What are schools *for* in a knowledge society?'

References

BECTA (1998) *Multimedia Portables for Teachers Pilot: Project Report.* Coventry: BECTA.

Bonnett, M. (1997) Computers in the classroom: some values issues, in A. McFarlane (ed.) *Information Technology and Authentic Learning: Realising the Potential of Computers in the Primary Classroom.* London: Routledge.

Buckingham, D., Scanlon, M. and Sefton-Green, J. (2001) Selling the digital dream: marketing educational technology to teachers and parents, in A.M. Loveless and V. Ellis (eds) *ICT, Pedagogy and the Curriculum: Subject to Change*. London: Routledge.

Covington, M. (1998) *The Will to Learn: A Guide for Motivating Young People*. Cambridge: Cambridge University Press.

Cuban, L. (1986) *Teachers and Machines: The Classroom Use of Technology Since 1920*. New York: Teachers' College Press.

Dawes, L. and Selwyn, N. (1999) Teaching with the dream machines: the representation of teachers and computers in information technology advertising, *Journal of Information Technology for Teacher Education*, 8(3): 289–305.

DES (Department of Education and Science) (1989) *Information Technology from 5 to 16*. London: HMSO.

DfE (Department for Education) (1995) *Information Technology in the National Curriculum*. London: HMSO.

DfEE (Department for Education and Employment) (1999) *The National Curriculum for England: Information and Communication Technology*. London: DfEE.

Downes, T. (1997) The computer as a toy and a tool in the home – implications for teacher education, in D. Passey and B. Samways (eds) *Information Technology: Supporting Change through Teacher Education*. London: Chapman & Hall.

Facer, K. and Furlong, R. (2000) Beyond the myth of the 'cyberkid': young people at the margins of the information revolution. Paper presented at the 'Virtual Society? Get Real!' Conference, Ashridge House, Hertfordshire.

Gardner, H. (1993) *Multiple Intelligences: The Theory in Practice*. New York: HarperCollins.

Heppell, S. (1994) Multimedia and learning: normal children, normal lives and real change, in J. Underwood (ed.) *Computer Based Learning: Potential into Practice*. London: David Fulton.

Jonassen, D.H. (2000) *Computers as Mindtools for Schools: Engaging Critical Thinking*, 2nd edn. Upper Saddle River, NJ: Merrill/Prentice Hall.

Lave, J. and Wenger, E. (1991) *Situated Learning: Legitimate Peripheral Participation*. Cambridge: Cambridge University Press.

Loveless, A. and Taylor, T. (2000) Creativity, visual literacy & ICT, in M. Leask and J. Meadows (eds) *Teaching and Learning with ICT in the Primary School*. London, Routledge.

Loveless, A.M., Williams, C.M. and Kutnick, P.J. (2000) Evaluating teachers' use of portable computers in administration and the curriculum. www.leeds.ac.uk/educol (accessed 15 Nov. 2001).

Ofsted (Office for Standards in Education) (2001) *ICT in Schools: The Impact of Government Initiatives – an interim report, April 2001*. London: Ofsted.

Papert, S. (1993) *The Children's Machine: Rethinking School in the Age of the Computer*. New York: Harvester Wheatsheaf.

Sanger, J. (2001) ICT, the demise of UK schooling and the rise of the individual learner, in A.M. Loveless and V. Ellis (eds) *ICT, Pedagogy and the Curriculum: Subject to Change*. London: Routledge.

Sanger, J., Wilson, J., Davies, B. and Whittaker, R. (1997) *Young Children, Videos and Computer Games: Issues for Parents and Teachers*. London: Falmer.

Scrimshaw, P. (1997) Computers and the teachers' role, in B. Somekh and N. Davis (eds) *Using Information Technology Effectively in Teaching and Learning*. London: Routledge.

Selwyn, N. (1999) Why the computer is not dominating schools: a failure of policy or a failure of practice? *Cambridge Journal of Education*, 29(1): 77–91.

Somekh, B. (2001) Research seminar presentation at the University of Brighton, April.

Stewart, T.A. (1997) *Intellectual Capital: The New Wealth of Organizations*. New York: Doubleday.

Sutherland, R. *et al.* (2000) A new environment for education? The computer in the home, *Computers and Education*, 34(3/4): 195–212.

Tomlinson, J. (1993) *The Control of Education*. London: Cassell.

Trilling, B. and Hood, P. (1999) Learning, technology and education reform in the knowledge age or 'We're wired, webbed and windowed, now what?' *Educational Technology*, 39(3): 5–17.

Wenger, E. (1998) *Communities of Practice: Learning, Meaning and Identity*. Cambridge: Cambridge University Press.

2

PERCEPTIONS OF HOW ICT HAS THE POTENTIAL TO INFLUENCE CHILDREN BEYOND THE CURRICULUM: HOME/SCHOOL/COMMUNITY LINKS

Toni Downes

Toni Downes' chapter draws upon two Australian research studies of the ways in which children and young people use information and communication technology (ICT) in their homes and in their schools. She highlights the contrast between the two contexts. Use of ICT in the home is described as exploratory, collaborative and 'just in time', and the development of ICT skills is related to a meaningful context for an individual, peer group or family. Use of ICT in school is described as constrained by different models of access to ICT resources, timetables, focus on skills and teacher direction. Downes discusses the experiences of children and their parents, carers and teachers, and raises challenging questions about the ways in which home/school/community environments can be informed by the salient features of each, which work well for children learning to deal with ICT in meaningful situations.

Introduction

Today's children work and play in a world where ICT is commonplace. Ownership and access to ICT in Australian homes, schools and communities has increased dramatically in recent years. While the number of computers in homes, schools and community locations has risen steadily, access to the Internet has followed an even sharper gradient. Data collected by the Australian Bureau of Statistics (2000) indicate that three quarters of Australian homes with children under 18 years of age have a home computer and half have Internet access. The proliferation of ICT in home and community locations has meant that many children interact with a variety of technologies on a daily basis. In fact, Australian children are more likely to use a computer in their homes than in their schools. Children who have access to a home computer use it for an average of one to five hours per week (Australian Bureau of Statistics 1998) compared with less than 30 minutes of access time allowed at school (Downes 1998).

It has been suggested that children learn better when there is congruence between the learning environments in their homes and in their schools (Toomey 1989). Given the trend of greater use of ICT in homes and communities, it is important for educators to narrow the widening gap between the learning contexts of home and school. Close examination of primary school students' use of ICT indicates a lack of congruence in the activities, purposes and processes in which they engage in the different locations. Strengthening the links between home and school has the potential for influencing and deepening students' learning with ICT.

For insight into the sociocultural contexts of students' computing I have drawn directly from data collected in two of my research studies. The first, conducted between 1995 and 1998, was a study of over 500 primary school students (children of 5–12 years of age) from a diversity of social, economic, cultural and language backgrounds who have computers in their homes. The study used a combination of qualitative and quantitative methods to explore how students use computers at home and at school and their experiences in learning with and about computers. One phase of the study explored students', parents' and teachers' perspectives on learning with technology.

The second study, conducted in 2000, gathered similar information to the first but used surveys and focus-group discussions with over 500 primary and secondary students (pupils of 8–18 years of age) from a non-government independent school which drew its students from an affluent community. The outcome is a rich picture of children's processes and practices with ICT at home and at school which is used to inform a discussion of how the home and school learning environments can align themselves more closely. Recommendations are made for how parents and teachers can best provide appropriate experiences and support for children's learning with ICT.

Computers in the home: the family context

In Australian homes the infusion of communication technologies has been so successful that they are generally considered to be part of the furniture and are fully integrated into family life (Apple Computer Australia 1996). Children as young as 3 are aware of the presence of computers in their homes (Fletcher-Flinn and Suddendorf 1998; Appropriate EdNA Services 1999). An average Australian household with children under 18 is likely to have a home computer and one out of every two of these households has Internet access (Australian Bureau of Statistics 2000). Affluent households are more likely to have two or more computers and associated peripheral devices such as printers and scanners and to purchase software regularly, compared with less affluent households (Downes 1998). Many homes have several computers which are designated for particular uses such as work or games, or for a particular user(s) such as mum, dad or the children.

The primary reason which parents give for purchasing ICT equipment is for their own employment-related work at home or for the benefit of their children. Previous studies agree that adults' use of computers in the workplace strongly influences the decisions they make about computers in the home (Dutton *et al.* 1987; Caron *et al.* 1989; Times Mirror Centre for the People and the Press 1994). Children who have parents or stepparents who use a computer in their workplace are twice as likely to have more computers in the home (Downes 1998). When discussing reasons for bringing computing equipment into the home, parents talk about its benefits for their children's education and for their future. Only children's discourses acknowledge the use of technology for entertainment. Parents accept computers being used as game machines provided there is some educational or recreational value in the games.

In addition to work, education and leisure, ICT is increasingly popular in homes for communication purposes. Parents and children talk about the speed and ease of accessing information and images with the Internet. Family members use email and chat software to communicate with family and friends and write letters for family and business purposes, and they are beginning to become more comfortable with shopping, ordering and banking online.

As part of the furniture at home, computers are located in common spaces such as family rooms, lounge rooms, rumpus rooms or the study. Being located in family areas offers children many opportunities to observe older siblings and parents using computers for a variety of purposes. The family home therefore provides children with opportunities for spectatorship and apprenticeship in which learning takes place 'on the job' by seeing and doing, and help is given 'just in time' when children are ready for it and are unable to go further on their own. When initially learning to use the computer or new software, children are guided by their parents and siblings. Family members use computers both individually and collaboratively to complete various tasks. There are times when the computer brings family members together in a joint activity – for example, creating a letterhead for the family business stationery or booking tickets for a theatre visit or an overseas trip. These types of project provide a constructive environment in which to learn how the technology works. It was the opinion of the majority of children interviewed that home computers are jointly owned by the family rather than owned by an individual family member (Downes 1998). This gives children equal status in shared ownership with the adults in the family, which is uniquely empowering compared with the situation of other technologies such as the mobile telephone or family car.

Not everyone in the family, however, is necessarily 'into computers'. There is often a 'support person' in the home who can help with initial learning and when problems with the computer arise, and there is also often someone in the home who rarely or never uses the computer. There were some comments that indicated that patterns of use in the home were related to gender differences. For example, in many cases the support person was male (dad or elder brother) and the least involved was female (mum or younger sister). Family rules indicate the priorities and limits of legitimate use. They define who is allowed to use the computer, for how long and for what reasons. Priority access is generally given to those wanting to 'work' over those wanting to 'play' and older family members are given priority over younger ones. Common family rules involve time limits for Internet use, chatting and game playing, how much paper can be used for printing and how expensive equipment must be protected by not consuming food and drink near it. Family rules provide strong messages to children about how and for what purposes ICT equipment can be used. With the popularity of surfing the Internet, families are implementing additional rules to protect their children from unsuitable content, exposure to sexually explicit or violent material, cyberstalkers and paedophiles, invasions of privacy, aggressive marketing, Internet addiction and sedentary lifestyles. Compared with school rules, home rules are generally less restrictive. A sense of shared ownership means that children have some power in negotiating extra time for practice and completing tasks. In most homes children are allowed to use the computer only after homework is completed, unless of course the computer is being used as a tool for doing the homework.

Children using ICT at home

Home computing environments offer children the potential to develop their skills through the processes they employ in the sheer variety of tasks available to them. The primary processes in which they engage are experimenting and exploring. Children talk about how well the process 'learning by doing' works for them. Many describe learning to use the computer and its software via the strategies of trial and error, fiddling, mucking around, just picking it up, practising, reading the help files and working it out for themselves. One child explained that 'You mess around and find out how it works' (Downes 1998).

Children also mention how they learn to use ICT by modelling from competent users such as parents, siblings and teachers. A typical comment about this aspect of learning was 'I watch my brothers and learn from their experience'. From observing episodes of others using computers in the home and drawing on their advice and assistance to fix problems, children are provided with positive role models for the use of ICT. Parents' personal interest and levels of expertise in technology are highly correlated with their children's, and directly influence the types of activity engaged in. Some children commented that what they learned at home they used at school and others said that what they learned at school they used at home (Groundwater-Smith *et al.* 2000). Transferring skills between environments appears to create a potential for greater learning.

When questioned about what they learn from using computers, children state that they learn about the technology itself as well as specific knowledge and information from games, CDs and the Internet. Some children perceive that they learn generalizable skills such as how to solve problems, how to think, how to have patience and perseverance and how to improve memory and imagination. As one child commented, 'When I research lots of things on the computer it gives me ideas'. Interestingly, some children contend that they are able to learn 'real world' skills from simulated computer environments, such as driving a car, shooting a target and playing sports.

Primary school children engage in a wide variety of computer-based tasks at home. The most frequently named activities were 'looking things up', 'typing things up' and game-playing (educational and other). Listening to music, browsing and chatting with friends are becoming more frequent with increased access to the Internet. Younger children enjoy using the drawing programs and educational games and sometimes make their own cards and posters. They talk about the programs they use in the language of play – for example, 'I can play painting and print my favourite pictures'. Even when using the computer as a tool for getting information, they use it as a 'playable' tool – for example, they talk about 'playing the encyclopedia'.

Typing up schoolwork steadily increases from Years 5 and 6 through high school, while game-playing decreases significantly around Year 7 (Groundwater-Smith *et al.* 2000). In the primary school years, children write and type up stories, poems and information texts for personal interest as well as for school. Information-seeking using CDs and the Internet remains high on the list of common activities throughout the school years for both school and leisure purposes. This is particularly so for the older secondary school students, who combine the tasks of accessing information and creating essays or reports with using the Internet for activities related to popular culture – particularly music, sport and entertainment.

Less common but regular activities include communicating through email and chatting with friends and family for leisure- and school-related reasons. Creating presentations for school or leisure and engaging in technical tasks such as downloading games, tools, wallpaper or documents, or changing desktop and software settings were reported. Comments related to instances of shopping online were infrequent and often mentioned in the context of using the computer with another family member. One or two students mentioned watching DVD movies, scanning images, booking tickets for shows and checking movie times online.

Overall, children's uses of computers can be classified into game-playing and non-game-playing activities. Gaming environments allow children to set their own goals and improve their performances through repetitive play. Children prefer games which have complexity, challenge, choice, elements of surprise, excitement and accomplishment in over-coming obstacles. In gaming environments they can gain control over the outcome of the game with consistent practice and in some games they are able to begin at the point they were up to in the last session. There is a degree of choice in selecting the game and the level of difficulty. In general, adults are not seen as the experts in game-playing and so games are relatively 'adult free' zones where children are given space and time to develop their own expertise.

Non-game-playing activities can be subdivided into four categories: creating texts, using texts, communicating and using technical processes. These categories are derived from focus-group discussions with children. The term 'texts' refers to cultural artefacts which are written, spoken, non-verbal, visual, auditory or multimedia communications. Children create and use texts for a variety of purposes. Creating texts includes the activities of composing, editing and decorating writing, drawing, design-ing, and constructing and manipulating images and sounds. Using texts involves locating, browsing, searching, viewing, reading, analysing and organizing information.

Children's conception of the computer as a playful tool has a number of consequences for them when creating and using texts. They spoke about using word processors to play with the 'look' of their writing. Word processors have the advantage of making it easier and quicker to edit the surface features of text such as spelling, punctuation and grammar, and make the work look better. Some children felt that word processors encourage creativity and self-expression in writing, and even encourage them to write more frequently and in greater quantities. In discussing the use of a computer for writing, children tended to focus more on the look of the text rather than the quality of the writing itself, such as its structure and vocabulary. One parent expressed the idea that 'Word processors can give you a better end-product but the intellectual component is the same'. It was not unusual for children, parents and several teachers to emphasize the presentation of the work over the content. This is not surprising considering the obvious and immediate feedback which occurs when fiddling with the look of text via a word processor. There is little, if any, immediate feedback when trying to improve the quality of writing.

When accessing information from a CD-ROM or the Internet, children search for texts with appropriate content which can be downloaded quickly or copied and pasted into a word-processing document. This leads to a focus on 'getting texts' rather than 'using texts'. They describe the ease with which they are able to locate the right information compared with searching through books and libraries. Many parents mentioned the convenience of not having to make special trips to the library. Electronic texts are easier to obtain and more interesting to look at, but they do not necessarily encourage children to make better sense of the information and use it or apply it in ways that incorporate it into knowledge. As one parent stated, 'It makes it [information] more accessible but it doesn't necessarily help'. Children still need to be able to read, analyse and paraphrase the information they obtain.

Using the Internet for email and online chatting moves computing from an individual pursuit to a more social activity. Older children report that they talk to friends, locate new friends and communicate with adults (extended family and professionals) for technical advice. The affordance of the computer as a communication device has the advantage of enabling children to communicate with people they would never have contacted with traditional technologies, and to gain an expanded view of the world according to parents and teachers. There are concerns, though, about the safety of children communicating and exchanging information with strangers and gaining access to inappropriate or harmful material.

A number of students commented on how the convergence of technologies has allowed them to achieve multitasking – for example, to complete homework while playing music CDs and chatting to classmates about the work on a chat site. Some of the older students spoke about how the advantage of working and playing simultaneously becomes a disadvantage if they get too distracted. Within the framework of uses, children describe episodes of activity where purposeful tasks are completed in playful ways. Using information texts can be playful, as in 'surfing the net', or purposeful in terms of looking up a web page of a favourite pop group or TV show.

Students, parents and teachers acknowledged the advantage of the computer as a productivity tool to make tasks easier, faster and better looking. One parent stated that 'It becomes very much a part of their life in terms of doing what they do – they play with it and use it as a tool', and another said, 'It's an everyday tool which she can use to do what she wants'. The fact that children feel they have a degree of control over the technology and can make it do what they want is identified as a critical feature of computing environments.

For the most part, children express high levels of comfort with their home computing environments, which include the physical resources, parents' and siblings' uses and skill levels, family rules and discourses. At home children learn to use ICT by having a variety of meaningful tasks available to them and having lots of time for engaging in the processes of playing, doing, exploring, experimenting and modelling. They develop significant competencies and confidence, because it's a part of their environment and they take these competencies to school. Children who don't have access at home don't have the opportunities nor the consequent competencies and confidence. This is emerging as a significant equity issue that needs careful attention for both social and educational policy.

Children using ICT at school

While many children first encounter ICT in their homes and communities, for those without computers at home the local school is a site where knowledge and experiences with computers can be gained. Teachers, parents and students believe that an important purpose of school computing is to provide access to, and skill development for, all children, but especially those who do not have a computer at home.

At school, computers are located in places such as computer laboratories, libraries, administration offices, staff rooms, resource centres and classrooms. They are not part of the furniture as they are at home, but associated with powerful spaces away from children such as executive staff and administration offices or restricted places where students can only enter with permission or when it's their turn. Most classroom teachers do not have a personal computer at school for their own use, nor ready access to sufficient numbers of computers when needed. Well-resourced schools have laptops or large numbers of desktops in a variety of locations and configurations. In these schools access to computers is generally very high, but still dependent on the teachers' decisions about when and how to incorporate them into their teaching. In schools with computer laboratories where all students are timetabled to use the computers on a regular basis, student use is regular but often infrequent (once or twice a week) and usually for only a short period of time – about 30 to 50 minutes. Where single computers are located in classrooms, libraries and withdrawal spaces, frequency of reported use drops to less than once a week and access across and within classes varies, such that some children might never use any computer at school.

Where individual classroom teachers hold responsibility for children's access to computers some inequities begin to surface. The children describe how they obtain access to the computers in their classrooms by taking turns. A turn at the computer is conditional on such things as completing classwork, asking the teacher, being chosen, waiting until the computer is free, getting there first and following a roster. Some children note that access sometimes relies on a teacher's memory. Students are aware of the tendency for teachers to use the computer as a reward for good behaviour or for fast finishers, thus advantaging some students over others.

Many students note that there is not a lot of time at school for practising the skills which are taught there and that those who don't have a computer at home miss out on being able to try things out for themselves and transferring skills between home and school computing environments. The practice of using software only once at school is in stark contrast to the way in which children learn at home through playing a game or using the software over and over again. At school, students are denied chances to improve their skills through their preferred mode of learning which is a blend of play, practice and performance. The average of 20 to 30 minutes of access time to school computers per week is rarely enough for students to finish substantial tasks in one sitting. The lack of time tends to influence some teachers into giving smaller, less cognitively demanding tasks which can be completed quickly.

Some schools have specialist technology teachers who manage (and control) the schools' responses to technology. For a majority of students, their sense of control over computing activity at school is severely limited compared with the situation at home. They are told 'not to fiddle' with the school computers and 'If you have a problem, ask, don't try to fix it yourself' (Downes 1998). One parent described the difference between the school and home environments in this way: 'They are freer to explore and discover at home, which is hugely beneficial, whereas at school it's a pretty tight sort of context, and so their learning will be fairly restricted'.

There was strong correlation between teachers' and students' reports of the types of task undertaken with ICT at school. Typical activities are 'typing things up' and 'looking things up'. There is generally less variety in school tasks and they cover a narrower range of skills. However, there are a few tasks which are unique to school environments, such as co-operative group activities, working with digital cameras, manipulating images, communicating with students at other schools, contacting experts and their organizations and creating web pages. Patterns of access and use are more related to particular teachers' interests than to systematic progression through a series of planned curriculum experiences. Older students comment that they are often expected to know how to use the technologies without being directly taught and that their teachers set tasks expecting that they are able to use the equipment with facility. This is a particular problem for students who don't have computers in their homes.

There were very few instances of students volunteering experiences of using computers for organizing or analysing information, for solving problems, modelling relationships, testing hypotheses or collecting data through input devices (e.g. measuring phenomena in science). Given that these are not common tasks at home or at school, conclusions could not be made about competence or confidence in these areas. In general, teachers report low levels of confidence in pedagogies for successful integration of ICT across the curriculum.

High levels of game-playing at school were reported by students in a minority of schools and this was probably because game-playing was embedded in particular curriculum practices – for example, educational games in the key learning area of *'Human society and its environment'*, one of the six key learning areas in the New South Wales primary curriculum (NSW Board of Studies 1998). Younger students sometimes find it difficult to distinguish between educational and entertainment software. It seems that in recent years using the Internet to browse and locate information for relevant units of work has taken over a considerable proportion of the time which used to be spent using educational games.

Computing experiences at school are often heavily teacher directed in order to achieve syllabus outcomes in the key learning areas or, at the other extreme, are superficial and tokenistic, such as typing up stories and playing games in free time. Some schools have highly structured skill-based programs in keyboarding which children generally find boring and lacking in complexity and challenge. In contrast to home, children are not allowed space to develop their own expertise and learning strategies at school because of the restrictions of resources, time and rules about playing. Modes of exploratory learning which are accepted by society as completely natural and appropriate for young children are rarely accepted in formal educational settings governed by greater numbers of rules. Even where genuine integration of various technologies into units of work does occur, skills are learned and used only once. They are quickly forgotten by the time students have a meaningful purpose for using them again.

Both parents and children believe that owning a home computer is advantageous for school performance, with 74 per cent of children stating that they do better at school because they have a computer at home. They feel that teachers give higher marks for assignments which are word-processed and well presented. Students, parents and teachers universally recognize the 'power' of the computer to make tasks faster and easier, to make work look better and to provide a greater variety of source material. However, teachers need to be constantly mindful of engaging their students in constructing and deconstructing texts to make meaning for real purposes, because preoccupation with the surface features of texts, such as font, style and colour, will not lead to deep learning.

It was evident from the research that the belief systems of individual teachers strongly influence how computers are used in classrooms. Many teachers still consider computing to be a marginal activity which is separate from literacy. Although computers are seen as important for the future world of work, they do not appear to be viewed as essential as having skills in literacy and mathematics. Both parents and teachers are concerned about the loss of traditional skills in handwriting and researching.

Congruence between home and school

Innovative schools have attempted to use the affordances of ICT to bring home, school and community closer together. The non-government independent school involved in the research implemented a systematic programme of increased communication between home and school using an integrated web-based school communication and information system (Groundwater-Smith *et al.* 2000). This system facilitates online communication between parents, teachers and students, enables the transfer of files between home and school and has discussion board and chat facilities. The software is loaded on to students' home computers and has the usual security devices. Teachers are able to post all homework assignments electronically and to communicate with students, their parents and other teachers more frequently. Students are able to seek immediate individual assistance, attention and feedback from teachers from either location. They can ask questions about the work while it is still fresh in their minds. Students can access their files to work on assignments from school or home computers. They do not have to worry about transporting disks and matching programs. They can submit assignments electronically and communicate with teachers and other students in discussion forums or by email. Parents can receive electronic reports of student progress. There was considerable evidence that the programme has been a positive experience which has assisted in growing expertise for all stakeholders.

It is clear that school computing environments will need to take advantage of the salient features of home computing environments which work well for their students. Working from children's discourses of how they learn best at home, schools need to create similar conditions at school. Comments made by one teacher indicate how children's ways of learning can be taken into consideration when teaching with technology: 'I don't want to have to teach them how to use all the things. I think they'll discover it for themselves – that's a teaching principle you'd use if you were going to give them any sort of equipment, you'd let them have a play for a while first. And then you'd start to direct them in the way that you want them to go.'

However, there is also a clear message from students that they require guidance and direct teaching at times and dislike it when their skill levels are assumed. Students emphasize their preference for watching and being shown and given assistance by competent models. Experienced models could be older students at the same school or from local high schools, colleges or universities, or visiting professionals. Having sufficient help available when needed for 'just in time' skill development is necessary when class sizes are large.

There needs to be plenty of time available for working things out collaboratively and individually and for practice to improve and commit the techniques which are learned to memory. Considerable blocks of class time need to be allocated for useful integration to be achieved. The idea of being able to work from home or school to extend episodes of meaningful activity is worth considering although there are obvious equity issues in that every student must own a home computer. Teachers need to view computing as a form of literacy which has equal value with traditional print-based forms. Students should be given tasks where they are engaged in making meaning for real purposes. From the investigations into the use of word processors it can be seen that students can be encouraged to give more attention to the content of texts as well as the look. Having a variety of tasks with sufficient complexity and challenge is a vital ingredient as generally schools offer a narrower, more convenient curriculum than is possible to achieve.

Features of home computing environments which could be incorporated into school environments are the freedom to explore with fewer rules, negotiation of time, availability of support persons, allowing students to set their own goals, and having a variety of individual and collaborative tasks with sufficient complexity and challenge. According to Walters (1999) a critical factor in teaching is to empower students so that they have more control over their work and learning. They thrive on experimentation and exploration.

References

Apple Computer Australia (1996) *The Impact of Computers on Australian Home Life*. Sydney: Apple Computer Australia.

Appropriate EdNA Services (1999) Commissioned by Education.Au for the *EdNA Online Pathways Project*. Prepared by Toni Downes, Leonie Arthur, Bronwyn Beecher and Lynn Kemp. www.edna.edu.au/EdNA/ (accessed 10 Sept. 2000).

Australian Bureau of Statistics (1998) *Household Use of Information Technology* (catalogue no. 8128.0). Canberra: Commonwealth of Australia.

Australian Bureau of Statistics (2000) *Use of the Internet by Householders, Australia* (catalogue no. 8147.0). Canberra: Commonwealth of Australia.

Caron, A.H., Giroux, L. and Douzou, S. (1989) Uses and impacts of home computers in Canada: a process of reappropriation, in J.L. Salvaggio and J. Bryant (eds), *Media Use in the Information Age*, pp. 147–62. Hillsdale, NJ: Lawrence Erlbaum Associates.

Downes, T. (1998) *Children's use of computers in their homes*. PhD thesis, University of Western Sydney.

Dutton, W.H., Rogers, E.M. and Jun, S. (1987) Diffusion and social impacts of personal computers, *Communication Research*, 14(2): 219–50.

Fletcher-Flinn, C.M. and Suddendorf, T. (1998) Computer attitudes, gender and exploratory behaviour, *SET Research Information for Teachers*, 1(8).

Groundwater-Smith, S., Downes, T. and Gibbons, P. (2000) SCEGGS Darlinghurst: information technology in teaching and learning – evaluation report. Unpublished report, University of Western Sydney.

NSW Board of Studies (1998) *Human Society and the Environment: K-6 Syllabus*. Sydney: NSW Board of Studies.

Times Mirror Centre for the People and the Press (1994) *Technology in the American Household*. New York: Times Mirror Centre for the People and the Press.

Toomey, D. (1989) Equality of opportunity, in P. Langford (ed.) *Educational Psychology: An Australian Perspective*, pp. 165–82. Melbourne: Longman Cheshire.

Walters, C. (1999) Teaching in 2000, *Learning Matters*, 4(1): 25–7.

3

LITERACY AND CONTENT: BUILDING A FOUNDATION FOR BRIDGING THE DIGITAL DIVIDE

Andy Carvin

The Benton Foundation is a US institution which works to realize the social benefits made possible by the public interest use of communications. Andy Carvin's chapter makes a distinctive contribution to this book in presenting a discussion of the 'digital divide' which focuses on issues relating to the wider community in which children are growing up, learning and attending schools. In any consideration of the use of information and communication technology (ICT) in primary schools, it is important to step back and analyse the range of factors which influence children's experiences, both inside and beyond the classroom walls. In a period when government policies reflect the priority given to ICT provision in schools, issues of equity, access and participation must be addressed. The digital divide is not a simplistic description of 'haves and have nots' and Andy Carvin's discussion highlights the significance of a critical and informed approach to key issues of literacy and content in the use of communication technologies.

Introduction

Over the course of the last several years, politicians and citizens alike have grappled with the public policy issue commonly known as the 'digital divide'. In today's digital economy, the question of whether or not you have access to information technology (IT) is no small matter

– by the year 2006, according to the US Department of Commerce, 50 per cent of all US jobs will be in the IT sector or will require IT skills. As it stands right now, high-tech workers make 78 per cent more money than the overall working population average. IT skills will continue to become an increasingly vital key to economic success: the more skills you have, the more advantage you and your family have in the digital economy.

The disabling hand of the digital divide stretches into our schools as well. The USA has started the process of connecting every classroom and library to the Internet. While the process is not complete, it is only a matter of time before all classrooms are connected. The wiring of our educational institutions has come at a significant cost: billions of dollars are spent on Internet access and education technology each year. There is no doubt that we have made a commitment to capitalize on IT as a learning tool, yet the divide still looms: only one third of America's educators feel they have the skills to integrate technology into their teaching, and most school districts only commit one tenth of the recommended funding towards professional development related to educational technology. Moreover, because of the access gap in US households, a significant percentage of students will remain at a tangible disadvantage because they lack the basic digital tools at home that their fellow classmates have.

Nor can we forget the impact that the digital divide has on our democracy: the Internet has become a tool of empowerment for everyday citizens, allowing them both the ability to collect the information they need to make well-informed decisions and to articulate their views in an open, public space. Denying people access to this information network denies them the opportunity to share their voices with countless citizens.

Economy, education and democracy are but some of the issues impacted by the digital divide. Yet in order to solve this divide, it is vital that policymakers, practitioners and community leaders agree upon a definition that clearly states its nature. It should almost go without saying: if we don't understand what the digital divide is, how can we be expected to develop a comprehensive strategy for bridging it? Despite this fact, too often we have relied on soundbites and clichés when discussing the digital divide: it's the haves versus the have nots, it's a digital gap, a digital gorge, a digital ravine. As easy as it may be to throw around these clichés in our public discussions, we cannot ignore our responsibility to acknowledge that the digital divide is a complex issue with no singular cause or effect. It is made up of a set of factors – some new, some long-standing – that must be addressed in tandem. Otherwise our efforts will be little more than quick fixes with no chance of sustainability.

The goal of bridging the divide is to use ICT to help improve the quality of life of all communities and their citizens, as well as to provide them with the tools, skills and information they need to help them realize their true potential. With that in mind, we can begin to discern the biggest factors that make up the digital divide. We have already recognized the need for better Internet access, for too many citizens lack the ability to access digital technology when they need it and where they need it. But we must also recognize the need for *literacy*, for citizens need a broad spectrum of skills in order to utilize ICT effectively. And we must recognize the need for *content*, since individuals and communities require a diversity of relevant, high-quality information – and the ability to create their own information – in order to become well-informed, publicly active citizens. By tackling literacy and content in conjunction with current attempts to improve Internet access, it becomes possible for communities to make sound policy decisions and forge strategic alliances for narrowing the digital divide.

Literacy

While much of the public debate concerning the digital divide has focused on access issues, it is vital that we bring literacy into the discussion as well. Imagine, for example, if every household in America had high-speed Internet access starting tomorrow. Would that mean we could wake up the next morning and celebrate the demise of the digital divide? Certainly not. As long as adults and young people lack the skills needed to use technology and information effectively, access is irrelevant.

It would be all too easy to pretend that the literacy issue simply boils down to promoting technology literacy – in other words, does everyone have the skills needed to use computers and other information tools effectively? Technology literacy is the one issue that seems to get the most play when people acknowledge a skills gap in regard to the digital divide. Yet the spectre of illiteracy can only be overcome by cultivating a broad spectrum of skills. When considered on their own, many of these skills may not seem directly connected to the divide. Taken as a whole, though, they comprise an arsenal of skills that allow each of us to combat the digital gap:

- *Basic literacy*: can I read and write?
- *Functional literacy*: can I put my reading and writing skills to daily use?
- *Occupational literacy*: do I know the basics of working in a business environment?
- *Technological literacy*: can I use common IT tools effectively?
- *Information literacy*: can I discern the quality of content?
- *Adaptive literacy*: can I develop new skills along the way?

Basic literacy. In the USA, basic literacy has always been high, yet we continue to struggle when it comes to introducing basic reading and writing skills to young people, especially in cases where their parents also suffer from basic illiteracy. Despite our efforts to make the Internet a true multimedia experience, the vast majority of online content is text-based. Such content is of little use to citizens if they do not have the skills to read it. Even in the cases where we've begun to develop compelling streaming audio-visual content that could be used to overcome literacy barriers, the irony is that the people who could benefit from it most – less-educated, lower-income families – are the least likely to afford the high-speed Internet access required to utilize it.

In 1997, former President Clinton called for the development of a grass-roots national strategy to combat basic illiteracy. The America Reads Challenge, as it is known, has forged a corps of literacy volunteers that help students improve their reading and writing skills. Over 2 million children have benefited from America Reads mentoring conducted by college students from 1100 universities. The federal government currently spends $260 million each year to combat illiteracy.[1] What can be done to link these efforts with pre-existing digital divide programs? For example, how can Community Technology Centres, catering to the needs of a given community or neighbourhood, partner with local literacy programs in order to offer a greater range of learning opportunities?

Functional literacy. In many ways, functional literacy is the secret shame of American education. While the vast majority of American adults are considered basically literate, the US Department of Education reports that nearly one in four adults is functionally illiterate.[2] Adults suffering from functional illiteracy lack the ability to apply their basic literacy skills to daily activities such as filling out forms, reading traffic signs, balancing cheque books or completing job applications. Adults, as well as young people, must learn how to put their basic reading and writing skills into context and utilize their skills on an ongoing basis in order to develop functional fluency.

Occupational literacy. As has been demonstrated in successful welfare-to-work programmes, citizens going into the workforce for the first time must become well acquainted with basic professional skills. These 'soft skills', as they are sometimes called, are tantamount to developing a personal work ethic such as going to work on time, dressing for the business environment and learning to engage with work peers. On the surface, these skills may seem as if they have nothing to do with solving the digital divide. However, if one of our goals is to give people the skills to use IT effectively in order to improve their economic standing, they must also master the skills necessary for participating in the workforce. Successful IT training programmes acknowledge the importance of occupational literacy by including this type of training alongside advanced IT training. Gaining skills as a certified network administrator, for example, doesn't mean much if you have no idea how to act in an office environment.

Technological literacy. Easily the most recognized skill set in digital divide discussions, technological literacy is the ability to utilize common IT tools, including hardware, software and Internet tools like search engines. Technological literacy is often a difficult task even for well-educated citizens, since it can be hard to break old working habits and develop new ones. The Ford Motor Company recently recognized the importance of improving the technological literacy of its workforce. Even though Ford workers are a part of the manufacturing industry, the way that industry does business has changed drastically and the Internet is now used for customer service and e-commerce, among many other uses. Ford, therefore, decided to give free PCs to all of its workers, plus low-cost Internet access. By encouraging its employees to sharpen their technological literacy skills, Ford hopes to improve the entire skill set of its company, allowing it to remain competitive in a changing digital economy.[3]

In the realm of K-12 education (schooling for 5–18-year-olds), technology literacy is an enormous issue. Two out of three teachers state in a recent US Department of Education survey that they weren't comfortable with using IT. It shouldn't be a surprise to any of us, though. Teachers on average receive less than 13 hours of technology training per year and 40 per cent of all teachers have never received any kind of IT professional development. To date, schools have not budgeted for proper training: though experts recommend that schools commit 30 per cent of their IT budgets to training, the national average is only 3 per cent. To make things worse, research from the University of California at Irvine's Teaching, Learning and Computing study suggests that teachers who are generally uncomfortable with interactive, constructivist engagement with their students are also uncomfortable using computers for teaching, even when access to technology isn't an issue.[4]

School districts simply must find better ways to support teachers when it comes to IT professional development on an ongoing basis. Similarly, a greater commitment must be made to prepare pre-service teachers for using technology. In the next ten years, experts predict a shortfall of over 2 million teachers due to an increase in retirements and a growing student population. The federal government has developed its so-called Preparing Tomorrow's Teachers with Technology (PT3) programme to do just that. With the recent change in presidential administrations the future of PT3 remains up for grabs and the need for serious pre-service IT training continues.

Information literacy. As more of us go online, it becomes necessary to develop better methods for expanding information literacy. Whenever we find a particular piece of information, whether on the web or on a bookshelf, we need the skills to ascertain its veracity, reliability, bias, timeliness and context. The Internet especially offers ne'er-do-wells countless opportunities to deceive and manipulate online users. Even when it comes to the millions of websites that were developed with sincerity and honesty, one cannot discount the need to be able to discern the potential biases associated with them. It is human nature for free speech to reflect personal agendas, so users must have the skills to put content into context. For example, a June 2000 study by the Pew Center for the People & The Press noticed an intriguing trend among consumers of news media. In general, users put greater trust in online news sources than print or broadcast news sources – even when the producer of both online and offline news was one and the same.[5] Our online society, and notably its young people, is placing greater faith in the quality of information they find online. Despite disturbing privacy trends in which companies profile Internet users without their permission, surveys strongly suggest that the average citizen would prefer companies to self-regulate their online activities rather than have the government impose regulation. No matter where the Internet regulation debate goes next, individuals will have to be prepared to gauge the quality of online information themselves. Developing fluency in information literacy is the only way to do that.

Adaptive literacy. The development of new technologies and the obsolescence of not-so-old technologies occurs at a dizzying pace. It often seems next to impossible to purchase a new computer or learn a new piece of software without the fear of a new release or upgrade looming around the corner. The key to succeeding in any environment that utilizes IT is the ability to develop adaptive literacy skills. While not universally seen as a type of literacy in a traditional sense, adaptive literacy is the willingness to learn how to use new tools and to apply previous learning to new situations. In day-to-day activities, such learning opportunities are usually incremental – from one type of PC to another or from one brand of email browser to another. The development of entirely new tools, however, forces us to make quantum adaptations in the way we learn and work. For example, even though the Internet has been a public phenomenon since the mid-1990s, Internet users and online publishers are still sorting out how to use the medium most effectively. Our adaptation to it is still in process. Nonetheless, other potential information revolutions are breathing down our necks – digital television and wireless personal digital assistants, for example – which means we're beginning another process of learning how to use these tools effectively as well. Adaptive literacy, therefore, isn't just a skill gained by individuals; it must be gained by communities, institutions, industries and nations as well. Groups and individuals adopt technologies at different paces, yet they must all take a certain amount of time to apply technology effectively before moving on to the next new tool. Our ability to harness adaptive literacy directly affects the pace at which we apply these new tools.

As can be seen, literacy as a whole is no single skill that is learned once and then taken for granted. Our abilities to read, write, work and learn improve over time only with accumulated experience. For individuals who are fully immersed in our information culture, it can be hard to separate ourselves from our own learning process, since so many of our skills are well established. But for individuals who have lacked learning opportunities in the past, gaining literacy skills is a daunting task, a continuous series of challenges. Our efforts to bridge the digital divide must acknowledge these challenges and integrate a range of literacy-building opportunities. Tackling literacy as an essential part of tackling the digital divide as a whole. Even though many aspects of literacy may not seem as sexy or compelling as technology or content, we ignore it at our own risk.

Content and the digital divide

The Internet is a revolutionary medium with no exact predecessors. Try as we might to find the right metaphor to describe its capacity (an information superhighway, a virtual railroad network or waterway system), the true power of the Internet is derived from the content that travels through it. More than ever before in our history of communications, ideas and voices can be shared from citizen to citizen, from community to community, with no centralized controlling authority dictating how information is transmitted. In effect, the power of the Internet is a function of the diversity of voices communicating through it. Nor is this power available only to certain groups. Unlike broadcasting, where information is produced by a limited number of media outlets and transmitted to the masses, any online citizen has the capability to produce content and share it with the rest of the world.

If we are to solve the digital divide, we must take steps to ensure that all individuals and communities have the ability to receive the content necessary to allow them to prosper – socially, economically and academically. And because the Internet is a multi-directional medium, we must also embrace the notion of citizens as producers of content instead of mere consumers of content. All citizens have the ability to contribute to their community in the real-world sense; the same notion should apply online as well. Recognizing that the Internet now contains literally tens of millions of pages of information, on the surface it may seem somewhat disingenuous to suggest that we are suffering from a content divide. But it only takes a little prying to discover the glaring information gaps that currently exist in cyberspace.

In March 2000, the Children's Partnership released the first major study of content issues in the digital divide.[6] Despite the enormous amounts of information available on the Internet, their research identified four specific areas in which content was severely lacking for many communities:

- *a lack of local information* – not enough community-relevant content;
- *literacy barriers* – content written for an élite audience;
- *language barriers* – limited non-English content;
- *a lack of cultural diversity* – limited resources for non-white audiences.

Along with these areas, one other dilemma must also be addressed – *accessibility barriers*. Examining each of these five areas may help to shed light on some of the work still to be done to bridge the digital divide.

Local information

The Internet has been quite successful in developing community-related content for large metropolitan areas. Commercial ventures such as City-Search, Digital Cities and other dot-coms have invested in developing commercial community networks where citizens of large cities can find information on local activities, businesses, schools etc. Such services also often provide discussion forums for local residents, providing an environment for community debate. Unfortunately, it's often been difficult for commercial community networks to scale downward to smaller communities, since their businesses require a minimum critical mass of local users and potential advertising revenue in order to justify entry into a community. The onus often falls on non-profit community networks to fill the gap and provide the capacity for smaller communities. In communities with a solid base of technology-competent citizens and the proper technological infrastructure, non-profit community networks often succeed. However, the overhead of maintaining the network and the lack of sustainable revenue often make it difficult for these networks to flourish in the long run.

Another angle some online services have taken to provide community content is the notion of online city directories – generic virtual templates that can be used to organize and promote local online content. Yahoo!, for example, offers Yahoo! Get Local! (www.local.yahoo.com), a collection of online directories representing thousands of communities across the USA. Each community's listing includes an archive of all known websites in that community. For example, Indialantic, Florida, with a population of less than 3000, has not merited the attention of a fully-fledged community network, but because the town contains numerous businesses, schools and people that maintain websites, they receive a listing in Yahoo! Get Local! While such services are a useful way of organizing pre-existing local online content, they offer neither increased online capacity nor a forum for community action. They serve as a disinterested directory of community content, but they have no direct interest in or experience of the communities themselves. In other words, as a generic directory listing service, they are unable to provide a true community perspective.

Several new online services may help bridge the content gap for small communities, though. For example, Out2.com provides a generic community newspaper template for over 10,000 US communities, including thousands of small towns. The citizens of these towns are then able to use the template freely in order to generate their own local online bulletin board services. Essentially, Out2.com provides the capacity for content-building and the community provides the context. Such services could serve as a model for allowing citizens to create relevant community content without having to invest in starting up a full-size community network service.

Literacy barriers

As noted earlier, an individual's literacy skills have a direct bearing on whether or not they can utilize IT effectively. This is especially true when considering how much of the Internet is text-based. Yet even in cases where adults would be considered functionally literate by any measure, there is the dilemma that too much of the Internet is written for a well-educated audience. This should come as no surprise considering the Internet's origins in academia – there was a time when only researchers and graduate students produced the lion's share of online content. Over time, of course, the Internet has become much more mainstream, with millions of citizens going online and millions more expressing interest in doing so.

Despite the changing educational demographics of the Internet, college-educated citizens still make up the bulk of online users, so content is written to cater to their particular literacy level. However, as an increasing number of non-college educated citizens are now going online, it has become necessary to consider what might be termed as 'literacy accessibility'. The federal government, for example, is required to make sure that all government content is accessible to a limited literacy audience. Other online services are not required to meet such guidelines, but nonetheless producers of online content must become more sensitive to the information needs of citizens with limited literacy skills. At the moment this means an openness to authoring text in ways that are easily understood. As streaming media improves in quality and affordability, audio-visual webcasting will offer new ways in which to communicate with low literacy audiences.

Language barriers

As of the year 2000, there is only a small handful of nations that are not connected to the Internet. From China to Vatican City, countries large and small are embracing the Internet's potential. A casual stroll through cyberspace, however, might suggest otherwise when you consider the preponderance of English-only content on the web. According to a recent study by the Spain-based Internet company Vilaweb, over 68 per cent of Internet content was in English, compared to only 3.87 per cent in Chinese, 2.96 per cent in French and 2.42 per cent in Spanish. Other widely spoken languages barely registered in the study – Arabic, for example, comprised only 0.04 per cent of all websites.[7] While the number of non-English sites is growing, it's not keeping pace with the number of non-English speakers who are trying to go online and take advantage of cyberspace. In July 2000, world leaders at the G-8 summit in Okinawa agreed to focus more resources on improving Internet access around the world. Unless the number of non-English websites grows with that access, we'll find ourselves in a situation where millions of world citizens will be unable to take advantage of Internet access opportunities.

Lack of cultural diversity

Related to the issue of language is the lack of cultural diversity in cyberspace. According to the Internet survey firm PC Data Online, the average Internet user is 33 years old, white, with a college background, and earns $67,000 per year. Even though the Internet has become more affordable to millions of users, in terms of content it's still a white, upper-middle-class experience. Some demographic groups are beginning to make important strides, though: a recent study by Cheskin Research suggests that Latinos are making significant progress online.[8] Businesses such as QuePasa.com and NetforAll.com are recognizing the potential of the expanding Latino market and are providing content of interest to that community.

At the same time, though, will the marketplace support the content needs of all minority communities? Probably not. Even in the case of Latinos, where companies are beginning to invest in content development, it's important to remember that not all Latino communities are the same: when you compare a tenth-generation Spanish family in New Mexico, a third-generation Cuban American family in Tampa, Florida, and a first-generation family of Guatamalan migrant workers in the Pacific north-west, you'll see that each group has its own content needs and expectations. Catering to all of them as being the exact same group of people only blurs the diversity among them.

Accessibility barriers

Lastly, it's important to address the content needs of the disabled community. There is a wide range of physical disabilities to contend with, and the majority of Americans will experience a temporary or permanent disability at some point in their lives. Just in terms of employment opportunities, having a disability can be a severe obstacle towards getting and maintaining a job. Despite our nation's current record level of employment, nearly 60 per cent of people with visual disabilities and 40 per cent of people with hearing disabilities are unemployed. Cyberspace has led to a revolution in American prosperity, but that prosperity has yet to affect the majority of people with disabilities, for too much of the Internet remains off-limits to them.

According to a March 2000 report from the Disability Statistics Center, only one quarter of the working disabled have a computer at home, and less than half of these people have Internet access.[9] It's quite understandable to see how few disabled citizens use the Internet, for so little of the Internet is readily accessible to them. The development of software that assists the disabled when accessing Internet content has long lagged behind overall website development. This has created a situation where millions of sites use technologies that are totally inaccessible to the disabled. Groups such as the CPB/WGBH National Center for Accessible Media and the world wide web Consortium's Web Accessibility Initiative are pioneering standards for website accessibility. Sadly, very few sites have implemented their recommendations, leaving an entire segment of our society barred from accessing the Internet and the content it has to offer.

Conclusion

Assuming we as a society are determined to bridge the digital divide, we must develop policies that tackle the issue as comprehensively as possible. Expanding Internet access to schools and libraries as well as to the general public has been an important first step, but it will be difficult to proceed without addressing the issues of literacy and content as well. Here in the USA, we must better shape current literacy programmes to interface with Internet access programmes and find new opportunities to encourage the expansion of public interest content. At the international level, the digital divide is fast becoming an important issue in developing countries, where the need for improved literacy and information sources is mandatory if any progress is to be made. If we ignore the importance of a better educated, better informed citizenry, all the Internet access in the world won't really add up to much.

Notes

1 See the 1998 Reading Excellence Act, as noted by the National Institute for Literacy (NIFL) at www.nifl.gov/lincs/collections/policy/rea.html (accessed 16 Nov. 2001).
2 US Department of Education (1992) *National Adult Literacy Survey*.

3 For more information on Ford, see Carvin, A. (2000) *From UUNet to UnionNet: Collective Bargaining and the Digital Divide.* www.benton.org/DigitalVoices/ dv020300 (accessed 3 Feb. 2000).

4 National Center for Education Statistics (1999) *Teacher Use of Computers and the Internet in Public Schools.* <http://nces.ed.gov/pubs2000/2000090.pdf. Becker, H.J. (1999) *Internet Use by Teachers.* www.crito.uci.edu/TLC/FINDINGS/internet-use/ (accessed 12 Feb. 1999).

5 Pew Center for the People and the Press (undated) *Internet Sapping Broadcast News Audience.* www.people-press.org/media00rpt.htm (accessed 16 Nov. 2001).

6 Children's Partnership (undated) *Online Content for Low-Income and Underserved Americans: The Digital Divide's New Frontier.* www.ChildrensPartnership.org/pub/ low_income/index.html (accessed 16 Nov. 2001).

7 Vilaweb, by way of Internet.com CyberAtlas. www.cyberatlas.internet.com/.

8 PC Data Online (2000) *Net Portrait Study, 1st Quarter 2000.* www.pcdataonline. com/press/pcdo042600.asp. Cheskin Research (2000) *The Digital World of Hispanics in the United States.* www.cheskin.com (accessed April 2000).

9 Stephen Kaye, H. (Disability Statistics Center) (2000) *Computer and Internet Use among People with Disabilities.* www.dsc.ucsf.edu (accessed March 2000).

4

FROM WEAK SIGNALS TO THE CONCEPT OF mLEARNING: THE LIVE PROJECT REVISITED

Janne Sariola, Aarno Rönkä,
Seppo Tella and Heikki Kynäslahti

The experiences described and discussed in this chapter reflect many aspects of the work of Janne Sariola and his colleagues in the University of Helsinki, Finland. They discuss a Finnish research and development project which anticipated the current emergence of mobile learning. In this project, called LIVE, pupils, teachers and student teachers used mobile telephony in an experiential and collaborative manner, working in direct contact with the surrounding community and with people in other parts of the country. They describe the everyday educational activities and elaborate on the concept of 'mLearning'. They argue that the project helped to combine pedagogical innovation and technological innovation which, in turn, contributed to the emergence of social innovation. Their starting point is the notion of weak signals.

Introduction: the weak signals of mLearning

Weak signals is a notion that was originally used in radio astronomy to provide visual evidence of barely noticeable signals over a fairly large frequency range. Lately, however, it has been used to refer to weak signs that are around us and that later are likely to become important trends or phenomena. The majority of people usually do not notice these signals, but some perspicacious persons might be able to 'sense' them. Weak signals are often on centre stage when information and communication technology (ICT) is incorporated into education.

This was the case in the Finnish LIVE (Learning in a Virtual School Environment) Project,[1] an example of innovative initiatives in Finnish school practices, coordinated by the University of Helsinki Media Education Centre[2] in the mid- to late-1990s. Certain weak signals were noticed, recognized and utilized by the LIVE team. These signals gradually grew into the concept of mobile learning or, simply, mLearning.

Background to LIVE: enhancing the quality of school education

School: a special place and time for people

Traditionally, some outer-world elements are brought into the school. Pupils read books, tell and listen to stories, look at pictures or videotapes, for instance, when considering what life is like outside school. Lauren Resnick (1987) argues in *Learning in School and Out* that a school is 'a special place and time for people', and that there is a specific discontinuance between school and people's daily lives. She claims that learning is often symbol-based in school, while outside actions are intimately connected with objects and events. In school, Resnick contends, isolated activities take place using symbols which are divorced from experience. When we think of the tools with which outside reality is brought into the school, we notice that these tools are artefacts of delay. Take books, for instance. They were written at least one year earlier. Pictures and slides shown in the school were taken the week before or five years ago. A lot of activities in school take place after a certain delay. Even narratives that are told in school often reveal a past character: 'When I was in Stockholm . . .', 'When our school visited the Houses of Parliament . . .'. Even things that are happening outside of school, at the very moment they are being talked about, are often treated in the past tense. The question then is about a certain kind of simulation geared towards things of the past. Outside reality is rebuilt inside the walls of a school by using images and symbols through abstraction from the real context and current time (Kynäslahti 1998).

Another point related to temporal and spatial considerations deals with going and coming. It is not unusual that pupils and teachers go outside the school to study things. Excursions are a traditional way to organize school work. But, we could argue, excursions also manifest a feeling of going and coming back. Often, but not always, things are not merely studied in the field, but on returning to the school. People go out to make observations, to interview people or to sample material, which they bring back to the school. After the excursion, these materials are processed and experiences discussed inside the four walls of a classroom: 'What did we see on our trip . . . ?' Again, the world outside is brought into the school with a certain delay.

When discussing the development of school and classroom, Reid (1990) reveals how, as organizational settings, they have been 'inventions' of their time, reflecting larger social developments. As an invention, the school 'has to fit with theories of practice and with social relations and conventions. More than this, as an educational invention, it has to mesh with the meanings which the world outside schools projects upon it' (Reid 1990: 210).

In the field of open and distance learning (ODL), a lively debate has flourished about Fordism and post-Fordism (e.g. Farnes 1993). In the LIVE context, the traditional school has been treated as a feature of modern society – more or less a Fordist feature. Projects such as LIVE are examples of development in which the school of the modern era is changing towards a new kind of school – call it the school of the information society, if you will. The separateness of school as a spatially isolated and functionally differentiated institution, isolated also in a temporal sense from the real life around it, is vanishing. The relationship between school and surrounding reality is immediate in LIVE. School becomes a part of the surrounding community, and the community merges with the school.

Virtual school

The current development of school as an institution has also been characterized by the concept 'virtual school', as the title of the LIVE project indicates. This concept is based on the wider notion of virtuality, which only recently has begun to be used in English. In the context of the LIVE project, we regard a virtual school as a symbiosis of the traditional school, with its physical appearance, and an electronic or telematic dimension of a school. The latter has transcended the spatial reality and operates in spheres maintained by ICT. However, we do not see the virtual dimension as opposite to what is real. Accordingly, we do not want to mystify virtuality as a strange metaphysical phenomenon. Some theorists have argued that virtuality refers to something that is even more concrete than reality (for 'real virtuality' see Castells 1996; see also Slevin 2000). Virtual environments, although not identical to the real world, are real environments of their own kind. A virtual school, then, is a possible school that widens our understanding of school as an educational institution.

As we have described above, in LIVE this widening, enabled by the extensive use of ICT in general and mLearning in particular, contributed to the emergence of a new temporal-spatial characteristic of school, predicting something new and inspiring in the field of education.

The innovative milieu of
the Finnish pedagogical context

The Finnish educational system is characterized by academic teacher education. All teachers, including primary school teachers ('class teachers') take a master's degree. Teacher education is supervised by the Faculty of Education Departments of Teacher Education. These departments combine research and practice to enhance the quality of school education and to help schools develop in general.

The University of Helsinki Department of Teacher Education, together with its Media Education Centre (see research[3]), has a long tradition of research on media education. Its research and development projects have covered quite a few current issues, such as the use of ICT in foreign language teaching (Tella 1991), virtual school (Tella 1995; Nummi *et al.* 1998; Tella *et al.* 1998), electronic networks of schools (e.g., Kynäslahti and Tella 1997; Tella and Kynäslahti 1998), technology-based pedagogical innovations in science teaching (Lavonen and Meisalo 2000), classroom-focused distance education and the virtual classroom (Falck *et al.* 1997) and dialogic communication (Tella and Mononen-Aaltonen 1998). Recently, the research has focused on network-based education (NBE) and learning materials (Tella 2000a, 2000b) and the teaching–studying–learning (TSL) process, associated with ICT, as a framework for the theory of teaching and the didactic possibilities of mobile technology, including e-book (Kynäslahti 2000; Tella 2000b).

In the light of this innovative atmosphere, it may be easier to see that the researchers' minds were open, so to speak, to weak signals, like the ones that caught the LIVE researchers' eyes in the mid-1990s. It was then that a group of media educationalists took the initiative to benefit from the encouraging experiences that had already been gathered from the use of videoconferencing at the school level (Meisalo 1996). Another aim was to further develop multimedia education and mediated communication in a school context. The emerging potential of mobile telephony was discovered and soon harnessed to serve educational purposes.

The LIVE Project (1997–9) emerged from this theoretical thinking. It focused on using ISDN-based videoconferencing and mLearning in authentic primary and lower secondary school contexts. Mobile telephony was based on Nokia Communicators,[4] small cellphones that combine email, fax, the Internet, an electronic notebook, contacts, various converters, calendar, clock and other services in an integrated hand-held format. Pupils were trained to key in their notes in real-life learning situations and to send them back to school by email or by fax. Another alternative was simply to use the integrated audioconference function in order to have a live exchange of ideas between the mobile, nomadic 'field' group and the 'base' group situated in the school building.

Implementing **LIVE**: network collaboration and experiential learning

The aim of the LIVE Project was to develop pedagogically relevant models of networking in mobile telephony (Nummi *et al.* 1998). The models would enable the teacher and the pupils to use and develop their skills of information management and communication in collaborative and experiential learning situations. The project also included experiments to increase openness and flexibility in learning situations by using ICT effectively. A special emphasis was placed on mobile telephony, which gave new opportunities for real-time interaction between the school and the surrounding community.

Structure

The LIVE Project was carried out in the distance education network of the Helsinki University Department of Teacher Education, including four schools in various parts of Finland. In teacher education, student teachers could choose a practical distance teaching course during which they were familiarized with didactic media planning and collaborative learning methods and practices. Didactic media planning means the way the teacher plans their teaching by using the possibilities provided by modern ICT. Planning is characterized by media selection, which is based on the principle of choosing the media which best support goal-orientated learning. Didactic media planning begins with the analysis of the features of the new media so that the most suitable media are selected for the contents of each teaching situation. In practice this means versatile use of media in teaching, including various communication channels and interactive audio, video or graphics. In brief, didactic media planning supports interactive, goal-oriented, multi-channel teaching.

The teacher educators involved in the project also established their own development groups to experiment on virtual school working models. Thus, both teacher educators and student teachers were looking for new flexible ways to teach and study in a virtual school. Right from the start of the project, researchers and teacher educators also established a common research and development group to discover pedagogical innovations for a virtual school and to put them into practice with student teachers and pupils.

Three levels of LIVE

The pedagogical applications of the LIVE project were based on the concepts of collaborative and experiential learning. Pupils carried out collaborative projects in which special emphasis was placed on developing the skills needed for group work, communication and information management. These skills were needed in the flexible and mobile learning environments where the interaction between the participants was essentially mediated by ICT. The learning tasks were carried out according to the so-called LIVE working models, which consisted of three levels, based on the physical and social characteristics of the learning environment – i.e. how many different groups were involved, how communication and information management took place, or what kind of technology was used.

Level I: the physical and social characteristics of the learning environment

At Level I, the pupils' studying, carried out as collaborative tasks, was supported by the ICT-mediated link between the school and its neighbourhood or the surrounding community. First, the pupils checked their background knowledge of the topic and brainstormed ideas of their own with their teacher. After gathering ideas, the contents were selected and the common goals were set. By forming collaborative groups, the learners helped to construct a social network, which later grew into the virtual environment enabled by ICT.

The collaborative groups were divided into the base group at school and the field group going outside the school. The base group gathered and analysed data from the Internet or other sources of information, while the field group obtained real-time information outside the school. The groups communicated via audioconferencing, short messages or email. Studying continued later with follow-up discussions and reporting in groups and the whole class. Assessment was based on personal and group portfolios. Finally, the pupils presented their own strengths or needs for development in learning (see Figure 4.1).

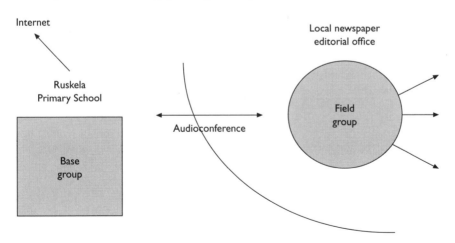

Figure 4.1 Level I

Case 1: visiting a newspaper office

A primary school field group visited the local newspaper office. Their aim was to obtain expert information about producing a newspaper. A real-time audioconference, with all participants listening to each other, was arranged between the pupils at school, using a conference phone, and the field group, using mobile telephony, and interviewing the journalists. If the questions of the field group were inaccurate, the base group at school were expected to ask the editors for clarifications. The role of the base group at school was especially active, as they were expected to support the field group with extra questions and comments. The teacher could facilitate the interaction by steering the discussion if necessary, but mostly she could stay in the background.

Case 2: LIVE in foreign language learning

On many lower secondary school class trips, which were made to Sweden, Germany, Hungary or Greece, a number of LIVE session experiments were conducted to extend foreign language learning situations to surroundings of foreign cultures. First, during the planning phases before the trips the participants agreed on the topics of the projects, ways of communication and timetables. The pupils on the trips formed field groups which communicated with the pupils remaining at school via integrated mobile telephony, using phone calls, short messages, audioconferences, email and faxes. The written communication, email and faxes consisted of pupils' questions and answers, descriptions, diaries and other reports. Phone contacts were highlighted by the audioconferences between those on trips and those at school, including real-time interviews of foreigners or reports of events and places. The projects ended with follow-up reports, discussions and assessment after the trips.

Analysis of Level I experiences

One of the main results was to evaluate the impact of experts from various fields who were invited to take part in the activities of the school. This created a competent discussion and innovation forum to satisfy the needs of the pupils, teachers and the whole TSL process and contributed beneficially to a symbiosis of virtual and physical school to promote the integration of the school and the surrounding society – a benefit of a virtual school, as argued by Tella (1995: 18). In all learning tasks, the collaborative planning phase proved important. With adequate collaborative planning, pupils got actively involved in working towards shared goals. When studying in a virtual school environment, pupils could communicate effectively via mobile phone in both real-time and time-independent (or asynchronous) interaction. Real-time discussions, interviews or reports via mobile telephony enhanced the possibilities for affective learning experiences and pupils' communication skills. It was also important to organize the activities so that both base and field groups could be actively involved in them. Finally, the analyses of the results and the evaluations of the activities were performed at both individual and group levels, including self-assessment.

Level II: how communication and information management took place

As a more networked model, Level II was based on using the expertise of two schools working in two subject areas, geography and history. The distance learning situation began with a common planning session between two schools via videoconferencing. The pupils of both schools had been divided into the mobile field groups and the base groups, which started to search and manage the project-specific information. The groups formed a four-point network in which communication took place via audioconferencing or email. Both mobile field groups transmitted information via audioconferencing and also collected the information they gathered into email messages to be transmitted to all the participants in the network. The role of the field groups was to serve as experts in their own network of learners. The base groups of both schools were connected via videoconferencing and e-mail, collecting background information and asking the field group for reality-based corrections or clarifications to their questions. The final learning product was a common report on the topic. A suitable topic was regional geography, with comparisons of the fauna and flora, ground formations, climate and local cultures of the regions to be studied (see Figure 4.2).

Case 3: LIVE in studying comparative regional geography

As part of LIVE, a comparative regional geography project was carried out between the Teacher Training Primary School and the Kilpisjärvi Primary School (located in north-western Lapland, 1200km north of Helsinki). The aim of this project was to increase knowledge and understanding of different kinds of living conditions. First, the pupils planned their visits via videoconferencing, considering specifically what kind of experiences or information could be interesting to the pupils of the other school. The home regions of the pupils differed significantly, as the pupils in Helsinki lived in metropolitan surroundings, while the home setting of the Kilpisjärvi school was a small, geographically isolated village in the middle of fells.

A city square and a fell with its surroundings were selected for the subject of comparison. First, a group of pupils at Kilpisjärvi went to a nearby fell, carrying a mobile communicator. While walking, they described their surroundings via the mobile phone. The pupils in Helsinki, hearing the description, drew pictures of the surroundings based on the audio description. Next, a group in Helsinki went to a marketplace near

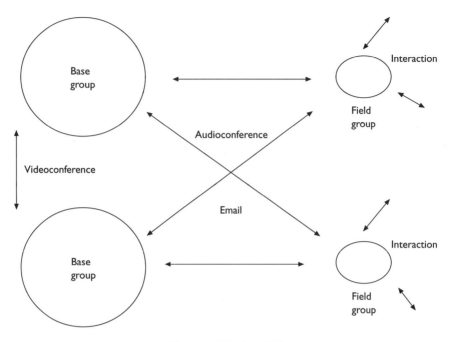

Figure 4.2   Level II

their school. They described shopping there, interviewed a stall vendor and depicted the surroundings of the square via a mobile phone. The pupils in Lapland drew pictures according to the audio description. After the two local groups had completed their tasks, they arranged a video-conference for the evaluation and appreciation of the pictures. They showed the pictures on document cameras, comparing their experiences. The mobile field groups could help make reality-based corrections to the pictures. Finally, there was a discussion about different living conditions and their effects on people's lives.

Case 4: a museum visit

Another comparison was made between the ways of living and the history of two different environments. A group of pupils from a primary school at Ruskela Village, not far from Helsinki, went to a local museum. Prior to the visit, the pupils had arranged an audioconference with the pupils of Kilpisjärvi, planning together the questions for the museum official. The interview of the official was arranged inside the museum, so that he could describe the things in the rooms and tell them about the local history. The interview and the descriptions were transmitted to Kilpisjärvi via audioconferencing. In self-evaluation, the pupils in Lapland wrote, 'Today we visited a museum!'

Analysis of Level II experiences

The pupils commented on how they concentrated closely on the instructions they heard via audioconference, because the descriptions took place in a real situation and were about things they had never seen themselves. Showing the pictures at a videoconference made things visible and open for corrections by the field groups, who acted as experts in the evaluation phase.

The essential feature of the museum visit was the mediated experience of the pupils in Lapland. The pupils in Kilpisjärvi had the experience of a real visit to the museum, 'seeing' the old things there because the interview and the descriptions were lively and accurate, adding to the affective character of their learning experiences. In our opinion, this was an excellent example of experiential learning as felt by the pupils themselves, showing the empowering impact of technology. The evaluation phase together with the teachers and the pupils of both schools contributed positively to the learning experience. Thus an extension from a local learning environment with the help of ICT to a more global environment provided new experiences. This is exactly what Tella (1995: 7) has argued: a learning environment employing ICT is characterized by expanding means of influence and communication, shared resources and possibilities of exchanging ideas and negotiation. This certainly seemed true in the LIVE project.

Level III: the kind of technology used

The third level embraces telecommunications in the form of interactive multimedia. With the help of integrated mobile telephony, it is possible to transmit text, pictures and photos, sound ('voicemails') and video excerpts ('videomails'). Pupils can shoot and record real-life situations on digital video and then transmit them to other learners in real time. For learning purposes, pupils can use audioconferencing or videoconferencing or the multimedia contents of an information network. They need skills and knowledge of audio-visual multimedia and their effects, for example, in selecting picture angles and planning the audio environment. Audio-visual presentation is the strength of videoconferencing. In addition, as Sariola (1996) argues, the video contact gives the teacher a better possibility to organize the learning situation, but even more crucial for the quality of teaching is the way the teacher and the pupils construct knowledge in the learning situation.

During the LIVE project, technology was not yet advanced enough, so not all ideas the researchers had could be implemented. The media tools for the third level are now becoming accessible. The latest mobile phones have features approaching those of multimedia personal computers. These integrated mobile communicators form an ICT bridge between the school and the outside reality. The greatest change compared to mobile learning on Levels I and II is the fact that producing information and learning materials in real-life situations has become easier, enhancing the self-production of materials in schools. In practice, this means transmitting video, still pictures and hypertext from the mobile communicators to a database, from which the information can be retrieved for further processing and discussion in learning. Thus the digital form of pupils' own authentic learning experiences makes the learning process more explicit, supporting the learner to understand their learning and helping the teacher to tutor the process.

Case 5: a not-too-futuristic prediction

Together, the pupils plan a biology project studying the plants and other organisms of the seashore. One group of pupils go to the shore, carrying mobile multimedia terminals. They take video pictures of plants and transmit the video clips via email to be further processed by the pupils at school. The pictures are saved in the digital portfolio of each group. During the learning process outside school, the pupils in the mobile group are tutored and supported via real time audioconferencing or video-conferencing. Pupils can also read the project instructions via the wireless application protocol (WAP) service of the group on their own mobile phones.

Case findings

The cases revealed a number of findings that were characteristic of the pedagogical nature of LIVE, as follows.

Prediction of future mLearning

The LIVE project included two basic elements: the prediction of theoretical models for mLearning and the testing of these models in a teacher education network. Predictions were not only presented in the theoretical models, but also in the new innovative ICT applications for mobile learning environments, which were planned and carried out by researchers and teacher educators.

Development networks to carry out and spread educational innovations

The innovative development during the LIVE Project was carried out on three levels of development networks. The first network consisted of the researchers and the teacher educators collaborating closely in creating pedagogical applications for the project. The second and the most extended network included the Department of Teacher Education and the schools. Because of the distances, the teachers and the teacher educators collaborated regularly in pedagogical discussions via mobile phones and videoconferences. The last network included the teachers or student teachers and the pupils, carrying out the study projects by using mobile telephony. These three networks supported and complemented each other in the innovative development work, which was characterized by the use of ICT to achieve effective interaction in the network.

Enhancement of experiential learning supported by ICT
By using mobile telephony, the pupils were in contact with authentic, reality-based events and phenomena outside school, which increased the possibilities of getting up-to-date information from the surrounding society through motivating and often highly emotional and intense real-time experiences, such as street interviews and museum visits, via audioconferences.

Development of innovative mLearning
This included the effective use of audio messages, short messages, faxes and email by the teachers and the pupils. Using easily applicable mobile telephony in teaching gave opportunities for mLearning in the neighbourhood of the school. From the perspective of student teachers and pupils this was small-scale distance learning inside the school area or its neighbourhood. This could be further developed into using other ICT tools, such as videoconferencing. Compared to ordinary classroom practices, mLearning implied a new kind of studying, which was active, experiential and collaborative.

Benefiting from outside experts in school learning
The combination of technological and pedagogical innovations in mLearning brought pupils in contact with outside experts and was also beneficial in changing teacher education practices towards openness and new kinds of network-based collaborative practices.

A basis for creating virtual learning communities
Through LIVE working, the local learning networks could be extended to a closer interaction with the surrounding community. This can lead to a better understanding of the processes of life.

The LIVE Project as a pedagogical and technological innovation

In educational parlance, innovation often refers to introducing and diffusing a new idea or method. The LIVE Project helped to combine a pedagogical innovation and a technological innovation. In our case, a pedagogical innovation refers to a constant need to change and update traditional emphases in teaching. Working in teacher education, we regard this as our first *credo*, and the LIVE Project emerged from our initial wish to combine pedagogy and modern ICT in an innovative way.

Technological innovations are usually designed by people other than educators. It is, however, up to the educators to find ways to adapt them for educational contexts and teaching purposes. In our thinking, technological innovations may lead to pedagogical applications and can further be used as educational technology to enhance the TSL process. Introducing a technological innovation implies strategic action, which is based on purposeful planning by the researchers in collaboration with the participating teachers.

A technological innovation can also refer to a process which starts from a new idea and ends with potential users accepting or rejecting the innovation. The usefulness of an innovation is clearly connected to the *milieu* in which it is being tested. In the LIVE Project, the technological innovation consisted of several new applications, such as ISDN-based videoconferencing and, more importantly, mobile telephony, which gradually led us to talk of 'mobile learning' or 'mLearning'. This new construct was based on the idea of allowing our pupils and teachers to make phone calls, use email and audioconferencing and send faxes and short messages through the Nokia Communicators. The Communicator was undoubtedly a technological innovation, completely unfamiliar to the teachers and pupils at the time of the project: a weak signal that was, however, recognized by the LIVE researchers. It may well be that this was the very first time, globally, when integrated mobile telephony was put into educational use in the primary school and made the object of extensive research.

In the next sections we focus mostly on explaining how the pedagogical innovation (our pedagogical thinking) and the technological innovation (the Communicator in particular) were merged by using the integrated mobile telephony. In principle, we believe that no consistent and differential influence on learning can be made by using any technology as such. More important are the ways in which contents are structured and conveyed. We argue that the approach adopted for the LIVE project highlighted and pointed to some new content areas, modes of pedagogical behaviour and ways of incorporating them into the learning process, thanks to a fruitful combination of technology and education.

The LIVE Project as a social innovation

Innovations are usually associated with change. Merging pedagogical and technological innovations can act as a catalyst that is likely to bring about change. We contend that when this kind of change takes place – for instance, when teachers change something in their teaching practices or methods of work due to adopting some new technology – the TSL process is affected as well. In the LIVE Project, the result of this change could be called a *social innovation* that had an empowering impact on the whole educational context in which teachers and pupils worked. A technological innovation incorporated certain media-specific elements into the TSL process, but was fully utilized only when the pedagogical thinking was guiding it. A social innovation always implies a new kind of discourse and new solutions to education, by adopting a societal perspective to the challenges encountered. In this sense, a social innovation makes full use of the combination of the pedagogical and technological innovations, leading to an enhanced and socially shared learning atmosphere.

Technological innovations also provide different domains of society with new channels through which further innovations can be launched into schools, offices and even people's homes. A social innovation means mental and social empowerment at the individual level, but equally with a view to the surrounding society.

The main focus in the LIVE project was on the synergy between the three different kinds of innovation: pedagogical, technological and social. When these three levels were taken into account and implemented in the TSL process, we believe this was bound to affect the societal level as well, leading to a societal impact generated by education and technology.

LIVE from the concluding perspective of communication and mediation at a distance

How did this integration of different kinds of innovations happen? Before answering this question we should return to the fundamental concepts of ICT: time and place. It is a current belief that the use of technology changes our traditional understanding of time in relation to place, and our comprehension of distance. One of the findings of the LIVE Project was that it wasn't significant whether the distance between the pupils and the teachers attending the LIVE sessions was 1km or 100km or, as it was the case in several sessions, even over 1000km. All these different distance options had similarities when working with mobile telephony in the school context. Admittedly, the distance had some impact on certain practical matters to be organized, but at the theoretical level nothing much changed.

Teaching, studying and learning in a classroom have traditionally been described as interactive processes. Interaction is naturally closely related to communication, which, in turn, is a fundamental component in school learning. Above, we argued that distance loses some of its significance as a substantial quality. What became essential in LIVE was the dimension of mediation. The notion of mediation has been promoted by technological advances, as communication is increasingly taking place in a mediated fashion, namely via technical means or through tools. Mediation means a relation between two things or two people (Quéau 1993: 21). The way people obtain information about the world and the way they handle it is fundamentally mediated. Wertsch *et al.* (1995: 21) argue that 'humans have access to the world only indirectly, or mediately, rather than directly, or immediately'.

Interestingly, in the LIVE Project, the concept of mediation grew into new dimensions. Let us first consider the everyday situations of the project at the school level – the 'LIVE sessions'. They dealt with pupils' working with mobile telephony in the school area, in its neighbourhood, in the surrounding community or between people in different parts of Finland. All these cases were concerned with the notion of mediation, regardless of the distance between the participants. Even classroom communication, often depicted as face-to-face classroom communication (everybody can see and hear the same things, everybody can be heard and be identified, for example – Tiffin and Rajasingham 1995) became mediated. However, some traditional features of classroom communication continued to exist. This symbiosis brought about a new pedagogical situation. Basically, the question is one of pedagogical innovation.

Mediation is often associated with indirectedness, as information about the world around us is not direct but mediated. In the LIVE Project, however, mediation also referred to direct information of the surrounding reality. This directness embraced several issues: temporal aspects, the notion of distance and the functional differentiation of school education from the societal perspective. In the final analysis, the concept of mediation dealt with two kinds of novel perspective in the LIVE Project. First, education was liberated from the physical restrictions of the classroom. This took place through technological mediation. In this mediation process, the nature of distance changed. In other words, the quantity of distance was not a determining factor for the mediated performance. Second, the boundaries between school and the surrounding society were done away with. The surrounding reality was in a mediated relation *vis-à-vis* the school. Equally, educational activities were spread outside of school through mediation. This change was made possible by innovative technological solutions – namely, integrated mobile telephony. This is bound to diminish the significance of physical location and the consequences brought about by the relations between locations, including distance. Again, mediation is a relevant factor. Pupils go out to the surrounding community with their mobile telephony devices, such as the Communicators in the LIVE Project, and mediate the outside world to the school.

The integration of pedagogical and technological innovations led to a social innovation that was represented, among other things, in the mediated representation of the surrounding community within the school, and the school within the surrounding community. We also noticed a change which we call the transition from the past tense to the present. The LIVE Project challenged us to reconsider the nature of the school as a place devoted to education, a place where the outside reality is processed with a certain delay.

When discussing ICT in different walks of life, including education, people often raise the issue of technological determinism: is it technology that determines social development or is it the people's needs that direct technological advancement? In the LIVE Project, we believe we found some solution to this notorious problem: both pedagogical and technological innovations dealt with the same kinds of issue, so, to some extent at least, they were convergent and in harmony with our educational rationale. In LIVE, in turn, this harmony was supported by our understanding of technological mediation and the new dimensions of communication – the C component of ICT – that became relevant and were conducive to meaningful learning.

The weak signals are still there

One of the aims in this chapter has been to illustrate how certain weak signals spotted in the pedagogical milieu of the mid- to late-1990s gradually grew into what we now call mLearning. One of its facets emerged from the technological mobility that allowed the pupils to study, in a more experiential way, outside of the school building, in a 'virtual school'. In LIVE, the participants worked in mutual and immediate 'real-time' collaboration, not only with the surrounding community but also with 'distant others' – that is, people from other parts of the country, contributing to the emergence of a pedagogically beneficial social innovation.

Weak signals are still around us, just waiting to be spotted and identified. To us, mLearning has been one of the constructs and phenomena that arose from spotting these signals. Even if it refers to mobile learning in the first place, we would like to think that the m- can also stand for mediated, one of our key words in this chapter. Thus, mLearning is not only mobile learning but also mediated learning. This interpretation, naturally, also calls for other interpretations. A weak signal is a weak signal is a weak signal . . .

Notes

1 www.edu.helsinki.fi/media/live.html
2 www.edu.helsinki.fi/media/
3 www.edu.helsinki.fi/media/research.html
4 www.nokia.com/phones/9210/index.html

64   JANNE SARIOLA et al.

References

Castells, M. (1996) *The Rise of the Network Society: The Information Age: Economy, Society and Culture*, vol. I. Oxford: Blackwell.

Falck, A-K., Husu, J., Kronlund, T. et al. (1997) Testing virtual classroom in the school context. *Distance Education*, 18(2): 231–69.

Farnes, N. (1993) Modes of production: Fordism and distance education, *Open Learning*, 8(1): 10–20.

Kynäslahti, H. (1998) What the LIVE Project tells us about the nature of the school, in T. Nummi, A. Rönkä and J. Sariola in collaboration with H. Kynäslahti, R. Ristola, S. Tella and A. Vähäpassi (eds) *Virtuality and Digital Nomadism: Introduction to the LIVE Project (1997–2000)*. Helsinki: Media Education Centre, Department of Teacher Education, University of Helsinki. Media Education Publications 6: 71–81.

Kynäslahti, H. (2000) Näkökulmia opetusteknologian käytön leviämiseen Helsingin yliopistossa: Opetusteknologiakeskus opetuskäytön edistäjänä [*The diffusion of educational technology in the University of Helsinki: The Educational Centre for ICT as a promoter of the use of technology in teaching.*] Helsinki: The Educational Centre for ICT, University of Helsinki.

Kynäslahti, H. and Tella, S. (1997) Collaboration of schools with distinct characters in networks of schools: in competition, connection, collaboration. *Proceedings of the 13th Annual Conference on Distance Teaching & Learning*, 6–8 August, pp. 169–74. Madison, WI.

Lavonen, J. and Meisalo, V. (2000) Science teachers and technology teachers developing electronics and electricity courses together, *International Journal of Science Education*, 22(4): 435–46.

Meisalo, V. (ed.) (1996) *The Integration of Remote Classrooms: A Distance Education Project Using Video Conferencing*. Helsinki: University of Helsinki, Department of Teacher Education Research Report 160.

Nummi, T., Rönkä, A. and Sariola, J. in collaboration with Kynäslahti, H., Ristola, R., Tella, S. and Vähäpassi, A. (eds) (1998) *Virtuality and Digital Nomadism: Introduction to the LIVE Project (1997–2000)*. Helsinki: Media Education Centre, Department of Teacher Education. University of Helsinki. Media Education Publications 6. www.helsinki.fi/~tella/mep6.html

Quéau, P. (1993) *Le virtuel: Vertus et vertiges*. Mayenne: Floch.

Reid, W. (1990) Strange curricula: origins and development of the institutional categories of schooling, *Journal of Curriculum Studies*, 22(3): 203–16.

Resnick, L. (1987) Learning in school and out, *Educational Researcher*, 16(9): 13–20.

Sariola, J. (1996) The planning of an open learning environment and didactic media choice in teacher education, in T. Nummi, A. Rönkä and J. Sariola in collaboration with H. Kynäslahti, R. Ristola, S. Tella and A. Vähäpassi (eds) *Virtuality and Digital Nomadism: Introduction to the LIVE Project (1997–2000)*. Helsinki: Media Education Centre, Department of Teacher Education, University of Helsinki Media Education Publications, 6: 23–49.

Slevin, J. (2000) *The Internet and Society*. Cambridge: Polity Press.

Tella, S. (1991) *Introducing International Communications Networks and Electronic Mail into Foreign Language Classrooms: A Case Study in Finnish Senior Secondary Schools*. Helsinki: Department of Teacher Education, University of Helsinki. Research Report 95. www.helsinki.fi/~tella/95abst.htm

Tella, S. (1995) *Virtual School in a Networking Learning Environment.* Helsinki: Department of Teacher Education, University of Helsinki OLE Publications 1. www.helsinki.fi/~tella/ole1.html

Tella, S. (ed.) (2000a) *Media, Mediation, Time and Communication: Emphases in Network-Based Media Education.* Helsinki: Media Education Centre, Department of Teacher Education, University of Helsinki Media Education Publications 9. www.Helsinki.fi/~tella/mep9.html

Tella, S. (2000b) Verkko-opetuksen lähtökohtia ja perusteita. [Initiating and justifying network-based education] in S. Tella, O. Nurminen, U. Oksanen and S. Vahtivuori (eds) *The TriO Project: Teaching, Studying and Learning Materials in a Network-Based Learning Environment. An Evaluation and Development Project of Network-Based Learning 1999–2000. Final Report, December 20, 2000.* Helsinki: University of Helsinki, Department of Teacher Education Media Education Centre and National Board of Education: 9–25.

Tella, S. and Kynäslahti, H. (1998) The emergence of electronic school networks. EDEN Annual Conference, 'Universities in a Digital Era: Transformation, Innovation and Tradition'. University of Bologna, 24–26 June.

Tella, S. and Mononen-Aaltonen, M. (1998) *Developing Dialogic Communication Culture in Media Education: Integrating Dialogism and Technology.* Helsinki: University of Helsinki, Department of Teacher Education Media Education Centre Media Education Publications 7. www.helsinki.fi/~tella/mep7.html

Tella, S., Kynäslahti, H. and Husu, J. (1998). Towards the recontext of the virtual school, in S. Tella (ed.) *Aspects of Media Education: Strategic Imperatives in the Information Age.* Helsinki: Media Education Centre, Department of Teacher Education. University of Helsinki Media Education Publications 8: 233–58. www.helsinki.fi/~tella/mep8.html

Tiffin, J. and Rajasingham, L. (1995) *In Search of the Virtual Class: Education in an Information Society.* London: Routledge.

Wertsch, J.V., Del Río, P. and Alvarez, A. (1995) *Sociocultural Studies of Mind.* Cambridge: Cambridge University Press.

5

DIGITAL HISTORY
AS RICH INFORMATION:
ACCESS AND ANALYSIS

Cheryl L. Mason
and David Hicks

Taking the view that 'history is an active and constructive meaning-making process', Cheryl Mason and David Hicks present a discussion, in a US context, of the ways in which information and communication technology (ICT) can be used as a medium for providing access to rich information from a variety of primary sources presented in multiple forms. The chapter addresses a number of issues about the experiences of learning and teaching history with digital resources for capturing, storing, analysing and presenting information. Using the Virginia Center for Digital History as an example, they demonstrate the ways in which pupils can 'do history' when they access and engage with primary sources such as letters, photographs, newspaper accounts and official records, to help them follow lines of enquiry which answer some questions and raise others. The role of the teacher in supporting pupils in their use of connected resources and modelling approaches to thinking with such rich resources is discussed. The context of these experiences is clearly embedded in the history curriculum in the USA, yet for readers in other countries addressing other curricula, it clearly illustrates key issues and principles of access and analysis when making meaning with sources of rich information.

Introduction

'Easily the most boring class was History of Magic, which was the only one taught by a ghost. Professor Binns had been very old indeed when he had fallen asleep in front of the staff room fire and got up the next morning to teach, leaving his body behind him. Binns droned on and on while they [the students] scribbled down names and dates, and got Emeric the Evil and Uric the Oddball mixed up' (Rowling 1997: 133).

For the likes of Harry Potter and his compatriots, history lessons at Hogwarts School of Witchcraft and Wizardry took the form of brain-deadening encounters with a subject that appeared devoid of enquiry, imagination, interpretation, conflict or personal meaning. Such a genre of history teaching, however, is not only the stuff of fiction. In fact, the teaching and learning of history as an officially sanctioned narrative of famous people and generative events continues to be observed by generations of students and detailed in many research reports as representing the typical state of history teaching in America (Baxter *et al.* 1964; Wiley and Race 1977; Shaver *et al.* 1979; Goodlad 1984; Ravitch and Finn 1987; Newmann 1991).

A growing number of history educators and researchers, grounded in theories of cognitive science and current socioconstructivist approaches to learning, argue that presenting history as a decontextualized, reified, 'rudely stamp'd' yet neatly packaged chronicle of facts fails to recognize the dynamic, fluid and complex nature of the subject (Jenkins 1991; Husbands 1996; Epstein 1997; Levstik 1997; Sexias 1997; Lee 1998; Hicks 1999; Levstik and Barton 2001). If school history is to go beyond a reductionist affair of 'telling' and being told, it becomes important for teachers, teacher educators, historians and policymakers to explore what history could become in our classrooms. This begins with recognizing that history is an active and constructive meaning-making process through which 'each person's view of the past heavily influences his or her view of the present and the future; it shapes one's conception of what is desirable or undesirable, possible or impossible' (Urban and Waggoner 1996: xx–xxi) Levstik and Barton (2001: 14) contended that children, beginning at the primary school level, should be given the opportunity and support to participate in the 'doing of history'.

This means that students have to learn what it is to ask and answer historical questions – how to find information, how to evaluate sources, how to reconcile conflicting accounts, how to create an interpretive account. And students certainly must learn what the authentic application of historical knowledge looks like. They must see how history can explain the present and they must see this in the most authentic of ways – through the comparison of conflicting ideas about the nature and significance of the past.

The growth of the world wide web has the potential to support such changes in the teaching and learning of history by providing teachers and students the opportunity to reconstruct the past by asking questions and by locating and analysing historical sources on the Internet. In England and North America ongoing educational initiatives and funding have given priority to providing Internet access to all schools (US Department of Education, National Center for Education Statistics 1999; British Educational Supplier Association 2000; DfEE 2000). Such efforts mirror Becker's (1999: 32) contention that 'along with word processing, the Internet may be the most valuable of the many computer technologies available to teachers and students'.

However, while the web places vast quantities of information before every teacher and student, merely having access to a wide range of disparate sources alone will not transform the history classroom. Issues related to the reliability of information, the relevance of information to the school curriculum, the permanence of information and effective pedagogy continually confront educators who want to teach with the web. Efforts to address such complex issues in order to support and encourage teachers to see technology as a partner in the teaching and learning of history in schools are being currently undertaken by digital history resource centres, such as the Virginia Center for Digital History. This chapter will introduce and define the work of such digital history resource centres and examine their potential to support and transform the teaching and learning of history at the primary school level.

Digital history resource centres

Primary sources

In the traditional history classroom, students studying the American Civil War are presented with a list of causes, results and key figures to memorize. Seldom are these students asked to make sense of the long list of names and dates or given the opportunity to hear and read people's voices from the past. Unfortunately, typical history textbooks do not provide teachers and students with the range and quality of primary sources that allow students to practise doing history.

When children have access to the raw materials of the past, such as personal letters and diaries, they have the opportunity to read the private and intimate thoughts of individuals surrounding significant events. For example, the following letter from P.H. Power to his wife not only describes the Battle of Fredericksburg and his desires for the end of the war, but also touches upon his sadness of not being at home with his family for Christmas:

Dec 25th 1862
My Dearest Wife
I hardly have the heart to wish you a Merry Christmas this
beautiful Christmas Morning because I will know merriment is not
for you this day but I can and do wish you a happy day and the
same to our little dears, who I suppose must be content with very

meager gifts and very few sweet things. I thought of them when
I first awoke this morning about day. And wondered what you
managed to put in their stockings. Memory went back to the many
happy Christmas days we have shared together with them. Alas
will the good old times ever return again? And you and I with our
little ones dwell together in peace? I hope so. I believe so, but the
heart sickens with the deferred hope . . . I wrote you some account
of the great fight. But you will see from the papers how terribly
whipped Burnside was, and what a commotion it has produced in
Yankeedom. I think the sky brightens and our chances for peace
improve. But still the war may bring on another year, or event to
the end of Lincoln's term. It is as warm this morning as June.
And every thing bright. If I only was with you for the day at least
I would have a happy Christmas. We are invited to dine with Tom
Bullard. I must now stop. With love to all.
Very Affectionately Yours,
P.H. Powers

Letters such as this one provide students with the opportunity to make
meaning out of the past and to ask questions that lead them to further
historical enquiry. For example, students can begin to interrogate such
sources in terms of paying attention to the credibility of the author,
evaluating the context from which the sources came and identifying
agreements and disagreements across sources, in order to begin to build
an understanding of what daily life was like for a soldier fighting in the
war, or to explore soldiers' motivation for fighting and the significance
of battles such as the one Powers mentioned.

New technologies: digital resource centres

Traditionally, teachers' and students' access to primary sources has been
limited. For this reason, the authentic task of doing history was restricted
to university professors and their students. Technology, however, is serving as a catalyst for change in teaching and researching at the university
level. Academics are exploring new ways of using emerging technologies
to democratize the research process and to provide more meaningful
learning experiences for their students. Often, the products of their
explorations are housed with digital resource centres. A digital resource
centre is an online academic centre, frequently associated with an effort
to employ technology to transform or reconceptualize an academic dis-
cipline (Bull *et al.* 2001).
  These modern archives contain vast resources of thousands of primary
sources, data sets, multimedia files and analytical tools. More importantly, they contain the knowledge, interpretation and perspective provided by the university scholars who use these resources. Not only can

students access nineteenth-century letters and images from the American Library of Congress, they can access an interpretation of the meaning of the image by an eminent scholar in the field. Analytical tools also provide students with the opportunity to reanalyse data sets to determine whether they agree with interpretations in their own textbooks. Students can learn to examine data at first hand and draw their own conclusions. Many of the world's universities and libraries contain world-class resources of this type – methods and resources that are transforming college instruction, and, we believe, can also be used to elevate school teaching and learning.

At the same time, however, care needs to be taken in using the world wide web to locate and use sources for the classroom. The value of many resources on the web that bypass traditional editorial standards may be suspect. The Drudge Report (www.drudgereport.com) is one example, providing access to late-breaking news reports on the Internet, sometimes before they appear in the mainstream press. Yet in a number of instances, retractions of inaccurate or incorrect information have subsequently appeared. Teachers are also often faced with the issue of having students search for primary sources on the web. For example, a recent search conducted for information on the Holocaust using 'www.altavista.com' revealed there were 290,525 pages on the Internet dedicated to this topic. The description given for the top-ranked page on the Holocaust was described as 'Monitors and refutes the claims of Holocaust deniers. Link to research guides, organizations, Holocaust camps and Nuremberg trial details'. The second ranked page was described as 'Holocaust information and remembrance, including historical essays and source materials, photographs, interviews, and many teaching resources'. This leaves many teachers concerned about how to integrate the world wide web into their classroom when students may access information that is inaccurate and harmful.

It is our belief that identifying and using digital resource centres in the classroom will help address issues of reliability, relevancy, permanency and pedagogy. Textbooks undergo an editorial review process to ensure that the information they contain is reliable. The reliability of the information on the world wide web is highly variable. While the world wide web contains unparalleled quantities of information, much of it is not directly relevant to K-12 education. Despite the vast content, teachers often encounter difficulty in locating information that addresses a specific curricular objective. Teachers who prepare lessons based on information on the world wide web often encounter the error message 'URL Not Found' or discover that the website has changed. There is no assurance that a website will be available the following week, much less in the next year. From the point of view of pedagogy, technology is changing the way we teach and learn. Teachers must consider adapting old methods and developing new strategies to best meet the needs of today's students.

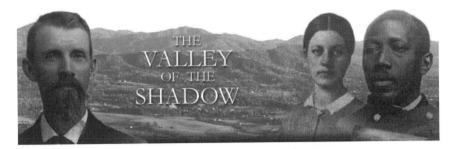

Figure 5.1 Banner from the Virginia Center for Digital History website (with permission)

The Virginia Center for Digital History

The Virginia Center for Digital History (VCDH) (www.vcdh.virginia.edu) is an exemplary model of a digital resource centre. The centre houses five digital archive projects containing thousands of primary sources. The projects, covering various aspects of American history, include 'Virtual Jamestown', the 'Virginia Runaways Project', the 'Dolley Madison Project', 'Valley of the Shadow: Two Communities in the American Civil War', 'African American History During the Jim Crow Era' and 'The Modern Virginia History Project'. The most extensive of these projects is the Valley of the Shadow. This hypermedia archive of more than 100,000 primary sources for the Civil War era contains newspapers, letters, diaries, photographs, maps, church records, population censuses, agricultural censuses and military records from two American communities, one northern and one southern, before, during and after the war. The National Endowment for the Humanities has cited the holdings of the VCDH as an 'illustration of the best that the web has to offer'.

These online historical resources allow college history students to employ the same research methodologies, working directly with primary sources, that historians themselves employ. Students can explore and examine many dimensions of the conflict and write their own histories, reconstructing the life stories of women, African Americans, farmers, politicians, soldiers and families. This resource has allowed history professors to reconceptualize the way in which college history courses are taught. Primary school teachers can also support and guide their students to use these archives to uncover stories from the past. Using digital history in the classroom allows teachers to guide their students to ask questions and learn about people, trends and events from the past through searching, discovering and analysing such primary sources. Not only does the Valley of the Shadow make primary sources accessible to the history and social studies classroom, it also allows students to interact and manipulate these sources to make meaning of them. Essentially, using digital archives in the classroom allows students to practise 'doing history'.

VCDH in schools

A team of educators from the University of Virginia has collaborated with classroom teachers to develop appropriate lesson plans to accompany the online digital history projects. These lessons attempt to incorporate higher-order thinking skills and to allow teachers and students to use the Internet in a constructive manner. One lesson plan example for primary students, entitled 'Dolley Madison and the War of 1812' offers a glimpse into the life of Dolley Madison often excluded from school textbooks. In this lesson, students learn more about the first lady and her life. They can uncover a letter written by Dolley that describes her flight from the burning White House and her heroic attempts to save the portrait of George Washington. This lesson and many others may be found at http://curry.edschool.virginia.edu/teacherlink/social/vcdh_lessons/

Most secondary history students in the USA are required to memorize the Gettsyburg Address. Yet very rarely is the topic explored in depth. What did it really mean? Why was it written? What did people of the time think about it? One lesson plan idea entitled the 'Commemoration of the Gettsyburg Battlefield: The Gettysburg Address' suggests that students explore newspapers, letters, photographs and battle maps available on the Valley of the Shadow website to reconstruct this historic event via primary sources. Links to this lesson plan and other lesson plans and concepts correlated with national history standards are provided on the associated web page.

Lessons such as 'Commemoration of the Gettysburg Battlefield' actively engage students in the construction and interpretation of American history. In this lesson, students are divided into expert teams to search for newspaper articles, letters, photographs and maps that provide contextual information about the Gettysburg Address. Each expert team uses The Valley of the Shadow database search engines to locate primary sources that relate to the Gettysburg Address. The students' searches will lead them to newspaper articles that describe the Gettysburg battlefield, days after the battle; lists of wounded soldiers and casualties; or perhaps a newspaper story that announces the order prohibiting the removal of bodies from the Gettysburg battleground during August and September due to health risks to wounded soldiers and local citizens. The search for photographs will reveal images of the battlefield in 1863 and images of Gettysburg, Pennsylvania today. In their searches, students will discover not only three-dimensional, geographically accurate maps of battlefields and regions, but also battlefield movies of virtual reality worlds. These movies provide an animated view of the battle over time. Additionally, students will locate soldiers' letters that describe the situations they endured. For example, Samuel Potter's letters to his wife:

July 20th 1863
Dear Cynthia,
. . . There are about 200 sick here. I have to act as Hospital Steward for them. They have not been in operation long & are not fully arrayed yet. The Drs. are very glad that I did come, as they had no one who knew anything about a Hospital Stewards duties & some of the Drs. dont know much about Hospital practice . . . Well we have driven the rebs back into Old Va. again & hurt them some as they were going. Our regiment had a brush with them while I was sick & several were killed & some wounded. Abe Lezarden was killed & James Milligan was wounded. I hear our hospital was a factory & stands high on the Virginia side of the Potomac which washes the walls of the building. The Stewards room has a window looking out on the river & I am writing this on the window seat with the roar of the river in my ears as I write. This is called the Factory Hospital & if you write soon address Factory Hospital, Ferry.

Near Sulphur Springs Va.
Sept. 5th 1863
Dear Cynthia,
Tell Josey if he wants to soldier put his cup full of water on the fire. Let it boil. Put in a spoonful of coffee & let it burn his fingers when it boils over & he tries to take it off. Then take a piece of fat pork. Get a rod about 2 feet long. Sharpen one end & stick it in the pork. Then hold it over the fire. The grease dripping will make it blare. Nicely roast his meat a little then put some water over it to wash off the salt which the fire draws out. Then hold it over the fire again & it is done & very good it will be to eat if he has not had anything to eat since yesterday morning. That is our style of cooking sometimes on the march. Then if he wants a bed let him go into a fence corner when it rains. Put a blanket on the ground, an over coat over him & an oil cloth over all & let it rain. We don't have it often that way. At Gettysburg we got to camp after dark one night & Dr. Miller & I made such a bed but happened to make it in a hollow. About 3 o'clock in the morning we awaked in about six inches of water & just remembered the old adage early to bed & early to rise so we thought we would rise early from our soft bed, built a large fire & enjoyed early rising.

Hyperlinked visual organizers are included for each expert team to help them identify and classify essential information. Once the students have identified the significance of the primary documents they have located, they are asked to hypothesize possible answers as to why, three months after the Battle of Gettysburg, did Lincoln choose to commemorate the battle? Each expert group shares information from their examination of materials. Students are then directed to a hyperlink that will take them to an online copy of the Gettysburg Address. Suggested questions are included for teachers so that they may lead students to uncover the significance of the Gettysburg Address.

The lesson entitled 'Substitution in the Civil War' has been created to give middle and secondary social studies students an opportunity to explore primary source materials from the Valley of the Shadow at the VCDH. This web-based lesson contains links to four letters and seven newspaper articles dealing with the issue of substitution in Augusta County, Virginia. During the Civil War soldiers in the South and the North could hire substitutes to carry out their military service. The lesson guides students toward defining and explaining substitution. Students are completely dependent on the primary sources at the Valley of the Shadow website to develop their definition. Consequently, students will construct their own evidence-based definition of substitution. Students also have an opportunity in the lesson to use their definition to determine the effect substitution had on the southern war effort. With adaptation by the teacher this lesson can be used as an introduction to historical methodology or as a vehicle for teaching about broader issues in the Civil War.

The VCDH is not alone in its efforts. Scholars and researchers from universities around the world are working to develop digital research centres for their teaching and research, which can be used in primary classrooms. Ideally an online digital resource centre that addresses reliability, permanence and relevance would have the following characteristics:

- The best digital resource centres reflect the use of technology to transform and reconceptualize university teaching and research.
- The work of the centre must withstand the test of peer review by scholars at other universities.
- The products and resources of the centre must have relevance to the K-12 curriculum (Bull *et al.* 2001).

Examples of digital history resources

We have selected the following digital resource centres as exemplary online collections of primary sources that can be used in the classroom. Each of these meets the criteria described in the previous section.

The *Perseus Digital Library* at Tufts University is a collection of images, maps and literature relating to the classical world. Resources are organized into art and archeology, student work, texts and secondary sources. Two thirds of the surviving literature to the death of Alexander the Great is housed here. Highlights of this archive include an interactive atlas of the classical world and a link to the Edwin C. Bolles collection on the history of London. The web address is www.perseus.tufts.edu A mirror site located in Oxford, England is located at http://perseus.csad.ox.ac.uk/

The *Camelot Project* at the University of Rochester is home to hundreds of pieces of art and Arthurian texts. Also included in this archive are bibliographies and basic information related to King Arthur. The web address is www.lib.rochester.edu/camelot/cphome.stm A mirror site is at the University of Groningen at www.ub.rug.nl/ozsmed/camelot.html

The *Galileo Project* at Rice University is an archive of resources depicting the life and work of Galileo Galilei (1564–1642). The main attraction of this project is Galileo's villa. Students may explore a hyperlinked image of his home to learn about everything from his scientific instruments to the Inquisition. Student work, an interactive map and a timeline are included in this site. The address is http://es.rice.edu/ES/humsoc/Galileo

The *Institute for the Advancement of Technology in the Humanities* at the University of Virginia is home to a number of developed online projects including 'Monuments and Dust: The Culture of Victorian London', 'The Salisbury Project', 'Uncle Tom's Cabin and American Culture', 'The Samantabhadra Collection' and 'Patterns of Reconstruction at Pompeii'. This digital resource centre is also home to the online scholarly journal, *Postmodern Cultural* (http://jefferson.village.virginia.edu/reports.html).

The *Convicts to Australia* site, housed by Murdoch University, is a collection of documents relating to the lives of convicts sent to Australia from 1788–1868. Although this site is intended for individuals interested in researching family history, students can use the archive to search the names and background information of those on the convict ships (male and female convicts and pensioner guards). The web address is http://carmen.murdoch.edu.au/community/dps/convicts/index.html

The Victorian Web: Literature, History, and Culture in the Age of Victoria at Brown University is a collection of documents from Queen Victoria's rule. The information included in this archive includes religion, art, literature, architecture, politics, technology and philosophy. The materials are searchable and cross-referenced. The web address is http://landow.stg.brown.edu/victorian/victov.html

Documenting the American South is housed by University of North Carolina at Chapel Hill. This project is home to five primary collections: 'First-Person Narratives of the American South', 'Library of Southern Literature', 'North American Slave Narratives', 'The Southern Homefront, 1861–1865' and 'The Church in the Southern Black Community'. The web address is http://metalab.unc.edu/docsouth/

The Lewis H. Beck Center for Electronic Collections & Services is housed by Emory University. A majority of these projects are either CD-ROM based or restricted to users at the university. Currently, there are five projects available to all users: 'The Merton Diaries Project', the 'Latin version of the twelfth-century cartulary of St. Aubin', 'Sermon at the Funeral of Dr. Martin Luther' – the first edition of Johann Bugenhagen's funeral sermon for Martin Luther, searchable database of articles from *Southern Changes*, a publication of southern regional councils, and the 'Women Writers Resource Project', a collection of edited and unedited texts from women in the seventeenth century through to the nineteenth century. The web address is http://chaucer.library.emory.edu/

The *University of Pennsylvania Library* maintains 'The Freedman Jewish Music Archive'. This collection is home to over 3000 Yiddish folk and art songs, theatre music, comedy and klezemer music. Students can review audio and video clips with accompanying text in both Yiddish and English. The web address is www.library.upenn.edu/etext/collections/freedman/index.html

The Rare Book, Manuscript, and Special Collections Library at Duke University publishes a number of online primary source collections. Among those that students can access are 'Historic American Sheet Music', 'Documents from the Women's Liberation Movement', 'African American Women', 'Emergence of Advertising in America, 1850–1920' and 'William Gale Gedney: Photographs and Writings'. The web address is http://scriptorium.lib.duke.edu/

The *United State Historical Census Browser* is housed at the University of Virginia and contains data for each US state and county from 1790 to 1960. Students may select different variables relating to American people and the American economy to research. The web address is http://fisher.lib.virginia.edu/census/

Identifying digital history resources based on these characteristics can ensure that the issues of reliability, relevance and permanence are met. However, the availability of digital history resource centres meeting such a criteria will not alone serve as the foundation for their use within the primary classroom. Whether a transformation in the teaching and learning of history will occur along the school spectrum rests with teachers' willingness to utilize technology as a partner within the primary school classroom and their informed belief that primary school children are capable of participating in digital history activities and research. Primary level children in England, while having varied experiences with information technology at home, feel comfortable using and playing with computers. However, a key question that must be explored more thoroughly is to what extent are primary level children cognitively capable of learning to think historically and ready to 'do history'? This requires an exploration of the literature related to the teaching and learning of history.

Teaching and learning history

Research on historical cognition has only taken hold in the last 15 years in America. However, Sexias (1994) pointed out that British researchers and curriculum specialists have been mapping the terrain of children's historical understanding since the mid-1960s. The development of the influential Schools Council History Project (SCHP) in 1972 initiated a series of research and evaluation projects examining secondary school children's ability to think historically (Booth 1994). The SCHP was founded on the philosophy that 'only by understanding history's propositional character (its "know that"), its procedural character (its "know how"), and its conceptual character (bond of these two) can a student begin to claim an understanding of the past' (Booth 1994: 63). The SCHP's design in terms of its focus on the development of historical skills and the analysis and evaluation of historical sources and second order historical concepts flew in the face of the research of the time, which concluded that adolescent schoolchildren, when working with historical materials, had only a limited ability for abstract thinking.

However, evaluation studies of the SCHP and an ongoing research base focusing on the development of young children and adolescents' historical thinking in England revealed there is no evidence to suggest that delaying instruction in history is developmentally appropriate (Booth 1979, 1983, 1994; Shemilt 1980; Ashby and Lee 1987; Ashby *et al.* 1997; Lee 1998). In fact research consistently shows that children of a wide range of ages and abilities are capable of abstract inductive historical thinking and can actively engage in the doing of history. What is clear is that children's understanding of history is a complex process that generally develops in a linear progression (Lee 1998). While age-related patterns of progress in children's historical thinking can be identified, mapping out children's historical skills and understanding into developmental sequences is much more difficult (Lee 1997, 1998; Barton 1998a). For as Lee (1998: 54) reported in his work examining children's developing understanding of the nature of historical accounts as they move through school: 'there can be a gap in understanding between students of the same age of at least seven years. A small number of 7-year-olds and 8-year-olds have ideas as powerful and sophisticated as most 14-year-olds, and a few 14-year-olds operate with ideas typical of 7- and 8-year-olds'.

A growing body of literature has now begun to specifically focus on primary children's abilities to understand history and think historically (Barton and Levstik 1996; Levstik and Barton 1996; Ashby *et al.* 1997; Barton 1997, 1998a, 1998b; Levstik and Barton 2001). Such work, similarly, contends that assuming children are incapable of developing an interest in history and an understanding of the nature of history before a set age is a mistake. Recent comparative research focusing on primary

school children in America and Northern Ireland supports such conten-
tions by revealing the importance of differing contexts of learning on
the development of children's understanding of historical time, the nature
and role of sources and the purpose of history (Barton 1998a, 1998b).
Barton (1998a: 60) contended that children's understanding of history is
not so much limited by cognitive factors as 'the nature and amount of
information they have at their disposal [rather, historical understanding]
is a set of skills educators can nurture, not an ability whose development
they must wait for or whose absence they must lament'. Such a position
supports the contention that the key to making school history a worth-
while experience for young children is for teachers to provide them with
the conceptual frames of reference with which to practise the doing of
history (Barton 1997; Lee 1998; Levstik and Barton 2001).

The move toward teaching the doing of digital history will require
teachers to conceptualize 'growth in students' historical understanding
as a progression of ideas [rather than] just an accretion of information'
(Lee 1998: 53). Within the primary school this means embedding the
available digital history sources, whether written, oral or visual, into
meaningful contexts in order for students to make personal connections
to the past and present (Levstik and Barton 2001). This will involve
designing clear instructional activities and materials that will guide
students as they imaginatively explore, talk about and connect to 'what
things looked like, what people did, and how they did it in the past' via
the rich array of available digital texts and images (Barton and Levstik
1996: 442–3).

Further research with young children (Levstik 1986; Levstik and Pappas
1987; Pappas 1993) reveals that teachers should not feel limited in their
choice of resources through which to begin engaging children in the
study of the past. This body of work suggests that both historical literacy
narratives and various information texts can be used within primary
classrooms to help young children develop ideas relating to the unfolding of events, which in turn can serve as a foundation to examine new
ideas and information from further sources. Conclusions such as these
support arguments for history classrooms being spaces where teachers
can actively engage young children in the 'doing of history'. Digital
history centres and archives can serve as one avenue through which
young children, with teachers as their 'expert guides', can approach a
wide range of easily accessible and appropriate sources and begin to
develop a personal and imaginative connectivity with the past.

Even with the resources that digital history centres can make available,
teaching young children to develop an understanding of the conceptual
character of history from primary school onward is no small task. Teachers
must recognize that learning history and developing an ability to participate in the doing of history will be an ongoing process. Both primary
and secondary schools teachers will have to recognize and accept that

students will encounter difficulties and develop misconceptions as they engage in the doing of digital history. This in itself is part of the process of learning, and teachers will have to recognize that the nature of the work students will produce will be an approximation of more sophisticated understandings (Pappas *et al.* 1999).

Suggestions that young children are only capable of providing slight and ineffectual levels of historical thinking and analysis ignore the point that, given a supportive instructional environment, history can become more than listening to a non-critical chronicling of the past in which knowledge is valued for the sake of knowing. For as Lee (1997: 48–9) contends, it is 'Absurd . . . to say that school children know any history if they have no understanding of how historical knowledge is attained, its relationship to evidence, and the way in which historians arbitrate between competing contradictory claims . . . Without an understanding of what makes a claim historical, there is nothing to distinguish such an ability from the ability to recite sagas, legends, myths or poems'.

Utilizing digital history centres within the primary school classroom to support teaching the 'doing of history' will entail adapting old methods and developing new strategies of instruction that go beyond the basic copying, remembering and reciting tasks that are reported to be the mainstay of the traditional classroom. Developing such strategies and materials for the digital history classroom can begin with the recognition that powerful and meaningful history teaching is always founded upon 'systematic and sophisticated literacy work, through an emphasis on audience and form, and properly underpinned by developing contextual knowledge' (Riley 1999: 12).

Doing history in the digital history classroom

Thoughtful literacy goes beyond the ability to read, remember, and recite on demand . . . if we focus children's attention almost exclusively on remembering after reading . . . they will confuse recall with understanding. And if we fail to provide students with models and demonstrations of thoughtful literacy and lessons on how to develop those proficiencies I fear that we will continue to develop students who don't even know that thoughtful literacy is the reason for reading.

(Allington 2000: 93)

'Thoughtful literacy' in the primary history classroom becomes an important concept when designing instructional activities using digital history sites. In order for children to develop the metacognitive knowledge and skills needed to ask historical questions, comprehend and work with ideas within various sources, and participate in thoughtful, self-conscious conversations regarding history, teachers will have to provide their students with appropriate reference frameworks and structures. The digital history classroom requires teachers first to navigate and guide their pupils in quests through layers of connected resources. Second, teachers must model for their pupils the manner of thinking and talking of historically conscious people. Because of these requirements, an instructional approach that has a great deal of potential within the digital history classroom is the 'cognitive apprenticeship' approach (Rogoff 1990).

Sustaining the concept of a cognitive apprenticeship in terms of developing a learner's ability to practise, as well as think about, the process of the doing of history, requires teachers to see themselves as part of an intricate network of experts, made up of historians, ICT specialists and teachers who are connected and partnered through time and space. Within the context of the networked digital history classroom, the teacher (the pedagogical expert) becomes a consistent provider of structure and guidance who is responsible for identifying, breaking down and demonstrating the strategies involved in the process of the doing of digital history while gradually giving the community of learners more responsibility and encouragement to contribute, articulate, practise and accomplish the same processes and strategies as their own competencies increase.

Initiating and sustaining instructional experiences through which children can begin to progress in their understanding of history in the context of the digital history classroom will require teachers and departments to consider their readiness and ability to take on the multifaceted role of network pedagogical experts. Taking on such a role, in terms of developing young children's abilities to develop historical questions, identify, collect and interpret appropriate digital resources and use such sources to construct a thoughtful, balanced and aware knowledge of the past, involves envisioning what the concept of 'thoughtful literacy' looks and sounds like in the context of the digital history classroom.

This begins with teachers asking such question as:

• How are the digital archives structured? Who developed the archives? Are they designed with the need of schools, curriculum, teachers and children in mind? How easy is it to search, locate and download sources for and in the classroom? What sources are available and how appropriate are they for the doing of history in the classroom? Will the site be available for future use?
• What ideas do pupils bring with them into the classroom with regard to the nature of history and the topic in question? What materials and strategies are available or will need to be developed to help students see how their understanding of the past changes over time as they continue to practise the doing of history using digital history resources?
• What broad narrative/informational understandings will pupils require as a framework if they are to remain focused, interested and motivated

to develop and explore historical questions using digital history resources?

- What key images, concepts and terms, within and between sources, will need to be drawn out, expanded upon, and discussed in order to make the sources accessible for students?
- What materials will have to be developed to transform a digital source (whether text, image or audio file) into an accessible and interesting source that can be interrogated by students?
- What materials and strategies will need to be developed to model how to examine and ascertain which sources are useful, and the extent of their usefulness in answering the historical question at hand?

Answering the first question involves a commitment on the part of the school and teachers to support and explore the utility of interactive technology within the classroom. Answering the subsequent questions will require teachers to consider adapting old methods and utilizing strategies and models to best meet the needs of doing history in the primary classroom. While such digital history sites as the VCDH have already begun or are in the process of developing specific lesson plans and materials to support the teaching of the doing of history based upon National Standards or Curriculum, a great deal of materials and strategies merely await creative modification by teachers. Graphic organizers, charts and discussion webs can provide insights into the understanding students bring with them into the digital history class, while also serving as a way for students and teachers to monitor their progress and understandings (Levstik and Barton 2001). Strategies, including Questioning the Author (Beck *et al.* 1997), and layers of inference analysis sheets for the sources (Riley 1999) can be reworked by teachers to provide their students with the chance to work carefully, consciously and cooperatively with digital history sources, and thus begin to develop the historical knowledge and evidential skills required for a balanced and rigorous exploration of the past.

Learning to teach and learning to do history within the primary school setting will take time. Clearly, teaching students to do history can and should begin in the primary school. Digital history centres, such as those detailed within this chapter, can serve as a reliable partner in transforming the teaching of history in schools. They offer the potential for teachers to model and provide their students with the understandings and abilities to engage in authentic historical enquiry, to access historical sources and data and to begin to make personal connections with people and places in the past like they have never done before.

Digital resource centres challenge teachers to begin to explore what history could become in the networked classroom of the new millennium. If we are not willing to examine such a challenge, to explore the potential of the Internet and, more importantly, digital history centres, the danger remains that history lessons will continue to appear to children to be nothing more than remembering what someone tells them about the past. Digital history centres in this sense provide the resources and networked expertise for teachers to choose between teaching 'history that is aware of what it is doing and a history that is not' (Jenkins 1991: 69).

References

Allington, R. (2000) *What Really Matters for Struggling Readers: Designing a Research Base Program*. New York: Addison Wesley.

Ashby, R. and Lee, P. (1987) Discussing the evidence, *Teaching History*, 48: 13–17.

Ashby, R., Lee, L. and Dickinson, A. (1997) How children explain the 'why' of history: the Chata research project on teaching history, *Social Education*, 61(1).

Barton, K. (1997) History: it can be elementary. An overview of elementary students' understanding of history, *Social Education*, 61(1): 13–16.

Barton, K. (1998a) 'That's a tricky piece': children's understanding of historical time in Northern Ireland. Paper presented to the Annual Meeting of the American Educational Research Association, San Diego, CA, 13–18 April.

Barton, K. (1998b) 'You'd be wanting to know about the past': social contexts of children's understanding in Northern Ireland and the United States. Paper presented to the Annual Meeting of the American Educational Research Association, San Diego, CA, 13–18 April.

Barton, K. and Levstik, L. (1996) 'Back when God was around and everything': the development of elementary children's understanding of historical time, *American Educational Research Journal*, 33: 419–54.

Baxter, M.B., Ferrell, R.H. and Wiltz, J.E. (1964) *The Teaching of American History in High Schools*. Bloomington, IN: Indiana University Press.

Beck, I., McKeown, M., Hamilton, R. and Kucan, L. (1997) *Questioning the Author*. Newark, DE: International Reading Association.

Becker, H. (1999) *Internet Use by Teachers: Conditions of Professional Use and Teacher Directed Student Use*. Teaching, Learning and Computing: 1998 National Survey: Report #1, Center for Research on Information Technology and Organizations, University of California at Irvine and University of Minnesota. www.crito.uci.edu/TLC/findings/Internet-Use/startpage.htm (accessed 28 Oct. 1999).

Booth, M. (1979) A longitudinal study of cognitive skills, concepts and attitudes of adolescents studying a modern world history syllabus and an analysis of their adductive historical thinking. Unpublished doctoral thesis, University of Reading, England.

Booth, M. (1983) Skills, concepts and attitudes: the development of adolescent children's historical thinking, *History and Theory*, 22: 101–17.

Booth, M. (1994) Cognition in history: a British perspective, *Educational Psychologist*, 29(2): 61–9.

British Educational Supplier Association (2000) *ICT in UK State Schools Survey 2000 (Executive Summary)*. www.besanet.org.uk/news/ict2000.htm (accessed 8 Nov. 2000).

Bull, G.L., Bull, G., Dawson, K. and Mason, C.L. (2001) Evaluation and using web-based resources, *Learning and Leading with Technology*, (28)7: 50–5.

DfEE (Department for Education and Employment) (2000) *Survey of Information and Communication Technology in Schools, England 2000.* www.defee.gov.uk/statistics/DB/SBU/b0197/index.html (accessed 6 Nov. 2000).

Epstein, T. (1997) Socio-cultural approaches to young people's historical understanding, *Social Education*, 61(1): 28–31.

Goodlad, J. (1984) *A Place Called School.* New York: McGraw-Hill.

Hicks, D. (1999) *Constructing Oneself as a Teacher of History: Case Studies of the Journey to the 'Other Side of the Desk' by Preservice Teachers in England and America.* PhD dissertation, Virginia Polytechnic.

Husbands, C. (1996) *What is History Teaching? Language, Ideas and Meaning in Learning About the Past.* Buckingham: Open University Press.

Jenkins, K. (1991) *Re-thinking History.* London: Routledge.

Lee, P. (1997) 'None of us was there': children's ideas about why historical accounts differ, in S. Ahonen *et al.* (eds) *Historiedidaktik, Norden 6, Nordisk Konferens om Historiedidaktik, Tampere 1996.* Copenhagen: Danmarks Laererhojskle.

Lee, P. (1998) Making sense of historical accounts, *Canadian Social Studies*, 32(1): 52–4.

Levstik, L. (1986) The relationship between historical response and narrative in a sixth grade classroom, *Theory and Research in Social Education*, 14(1): 1–19.

Levstik, L. (1997) Any history is someone's history: listening to multiple voices from the past, *Social Education*, 61(1): 48–51.

Levstik, L. and Barton, K. (1996) 'They still use some of their past': historical salience in elementary children's chronological thinking, *Journal of Curriculum Studies*, 28: 531–76.

Levstik, L. and Barton, K. (2001) *Doing History: Investigating with Children in Elementary and Middle Schools*, 2nd edn. Hillsdale, NJ: Lawrence Erlbaum Associates.

Levstik, L. and Pappas, C. (1987) Exploring the development of historical understanding, *Journal of Research and Development in Education*, 21(1): 1–15.

Newmann, F.M. (1991) Promoting higher order thinking in social studies: overview of a study of sixteen high school departments, *Theory and Research in Social Education*, 19: 324–40.

Pappas, C. (1993) Is narrative 'primary'? Some insights from kindergarteners' pretend reading of stories and information books, *Journal of Reading Behaviour*, 25(1): 97–129.

Pappas, C., Keifer, B. and Levstik, L. (1999) *An Integrated Language Perspective in the Elementary School: An Action Approach*, 3rd edn. New York: Longman.

Ravitch, D. and Finn, C.E. (1987) *What Do Our 17-year-olds Know? A Report on the First National Assessment of History and Literature.* New York: Harper & Row.

Riley, C. (1999) Evidential understanding, period knowledge and the development of literacy: a practical approach to 'layer of inference', *Teaching History*, 97: 6–12.

Rogoff, B. (1990) *Apprenticeship in Thinking: Cognitive Development in Social Context.* New York: Oxford University Press.

Rowling, J.K. (1997) *Harry Potter and the Sorcerer's Stone.* New York: Scholastic.

Sexias, P. (1994) When psychologists discuss historical thinking: a historian's perspective, *Educational Psychologist*, 29(2): 107–9.

Sexias, P. (1997) Mapping the terrain of historical significance, *Social Education*, 61(1): 22–7.

Shaver, J.P., Davis, O.L. Jr. and Helburn, S.W. (1979) The status of social studies education: impressions from three NSF studies, *Social Education*, 43(2): 150–9.

Shemilt, D. (1980) *Evaluation Study: Schools Council History 13–16 Project*. Edinburgh: Holmes McDougall.

Urban, W. and Waggoner, J. Jr. (1996) *American Education: A History*. New York: McGraw-Hill.

US Department of Education, National Center for Education Statistics (1999) *Internet Access in Public Schools, 1994–1998*. Washington, DC: US Department of Education.

Wiley, K.B. and Race, J. (1977) *The Status of Pre-College Science, Mathematics, and Social Science Education: 1955–75*, vol. 3: *Social Science Education*. Boulder, CO: Social Science Consortium.

6

ASDF; LKJH: CHALLENGES TO EARLY CHILDHOOD CURRICULUM AND PEDAGOGY IN THE INFORMATION AGE

Nicola Yelland

How might young children's experiences in a primary classroom reflect the potential for information and communication technology (ICT) to be an integral part of their learning in an 'information society'? Nicola Yelland presents a discussion of the challenges to traditional curricula and teaching strategies which are posed by the imaginative use of ICT by teachers. She calls for a reconceptualization of the curriculum in which ICT is used as 'an artefact of innovation'. In this chapter she describes a number of examples of children's learning with technology embedded in the curriculum and argues that ICT can extend the repertoire of good teachers and enable children to represent their understanding in varied and dynamic ways.

Introduction: the potential of ICT beyond the curriculum

ICT has fundamentally changed the way we do things in our everyday lives and in business. However, although this is evident all around us, schools and education policy seem to be caught in a 'time warp' and continue to adopt the practice of mapping the new technologies on to old curricula with tired pedagogy – in much the same way that we persist with the qwerty keyboard and start learning to type with asdf; lkjh. One wonders, for example, why we still have handwriting lessons? Why do children still write out projects, decorate them with pretty borders and colour them meticulously, and why are mathematics textbooks still full of 'sums' that children spend an inordinate time on, just to prove they know the method and can perform it accurately time and time again? These attributes were valued in previous decades and many still lament that they have had their day. It is generally accepted, for example in mathematics, that rote learning and pencil and paper computations should be de-emphasized while there is a recognized acceptance of the need to provide opportunities for students to engage in collaborative problem-solving experiences which will enable them to acquire and use knowledge as they encounter new problems in a variety of contexts (e.g. DETYA 2000; NCTM 2000). Such skills are appropriate to the information age. Yet, simply bringing computers and the Internet into the classroom will not result in the creation of such learning environments. In some cases it may mask the complexities that we, as a profession, have not addressed.

For example, I was in a classroom shortly after returning to Australia from the USA. The teacher of the class was a 'good' teacher who cared about the children in his Year 3 class. They had recently acquired a new computer with an Internet connection. One can visualize the policymakers boasting how they had every classroom wired in the State, but failing to check, or be concerned whether the teachers who had received these computers were capable of using them to search for information on the Internet. In this example the class were investigating 'endangered species' and I mentioned that I had just seen the new panda that was born in the San Diego Zoo, and that we could actually go to the site to see pictures of her. We brought the children together and set about finding the zoo site on the computer via the Internet. By following the links and with a good deal of common sense and help from the children along the way, we located the section on pandas and found a video about the newly-born baby panda. Everyone was excited! I mentioned to the teacher that the site was a good one and would be worth exploring in order to see what else was there in terms of the topic that they were studying. He thought that was a good idea and I showed him how to bookmark it as a favourite place. When I returned a week later he said that it was a good site and that he had downloaded several activities for the children. These included a printout of an armadillo which had been coloured in by each child in the class. This low-level cognitive task was no more suited to 2-year-olds than to this bright and inquisitive group of children who were 8 or just 9 years of age, and who had maintained a steady banter of asking intelligent questions as we first searched the site the previous week.

Another example was found in the next classroom when again, connected to a class theme, the group searched the Internet to find information associated with a cultural activity called 'Under 8s Week'. When we found the site we discovered it had more low-level activities. The children were required to select from eight items which ones they would take for their day trip to the theatre, and which would be rejected. While on the surface this might be viewed as a useful classification exercise it did not require the use of technology, let alone Internet access, and if a child selected an inappropriate item, such as a chair, there was no feedback provided to suggest why it was not to be included. When a suitable item, such as a water bottle, was dragged into the bag it had the same end result. Such an activity could have more easily been acted out in a class or small group discussion session, where the children might offer oral solutions for their choices, or be required to select a number of items from their own knowledge base.

These examples are not provided to deride the teachers. Without appropriate professional development opportunities they are not able to accommodate ICT in their programme effectively. There is a need for them to rethink the curricula and their pedagogy in terms of ICT – and they require support at the systemic level in order to succeed. New policies and funding need to be accompanied by strategies for effective implementation, including the development of curricula in which ICT is embedded, so that the use of computers is an integral part of the process of learning. Tinker (1999: 1) has contended that 'potentially revolutionary technologies have not been used to create fundamental improvements in the traditional sequence of topics'. Tinker continued by pointing out that if, by working in technological environments, students acquire knowledge in new ways, then the curriculum should build on that information. In this way the content and structure of curriculum need to be reshaped for the information age.

I have previously stated (Yelland 1999, 2001) five ways in which we can *start* to develop skills in teaching children in the information age. These are:

- the integration of technology and curricula;
- the promotion of active learning, enquiry and problem-solving environments that engage children in individual and collaborative work using higher-order thinking skills;
- the extended use of technology to present and represent ideas;
- new definitions of play and exploration and the redefinition of what constitutes 'a manipulative' as a guide for learning;
- the development of media literacy skills that involve a critical analysis of the use of technologies and the information derived from them.

This chapter will highlight some issues related to learning in the early childhood years and then address new examples of exploring and learning with technology to demonstrate the powerful ways in which computers can engage children in learning and knowledge acquisition. The examples will also demonstrate collaborative learning in computer contexts where the use of scaffolding by the teacher is essential for cognitive growth.

Early childhood education

It is a long held belief in early childhood education that young children learn best in an environment characterized by play. An essential component of this is the notion that children need to explore elements in their world using all their senses, via hands-on experiences. ICT is viewed as a challenge to this fundamental belief and as a threat to play in the real world. Yet most advocates of the use of computers by young children basically promote the use of technology as another medium by which children can explore and solve problems and agree that it is essential for children to regularly interact with three-dimensional materials (Clements and Nastasi 1992). Such educators view computer activities with good software as providing opportunities to extend thinking in a different mode that will ultimately enhance the ways in which young children make sense of ideas and communicate their understandings to others (Clements 1994).

Computers are very much a part of many young children's lives. A report by the Kaiser Family Foundation (1999) entitled *Kids and Media: The New Millennium* highlighted the large amount of time that children spend interacting with media. Yet interestingly this tended to be traditional media, like television, rather than computers. In fact, they reported that children in the age group of 2 to 18 years only spent about half an hour a day using computers, including the use of computers in school time. They spent 21 minutes on average using computers for 'fun' while they spent two and three quarter hours watching television. Approximately 9 per cent of the children surveyed spent more than an hour a day using computers for fun and only 3 per cent spent more than an hour online each day. Thus, the perception of children spending inordinate amounts of time at the computer, to the detriment of other more physical pursuits, and developing poor health and repetitive strain injury as a consequence (as reported by the Alliance for Childhood 2000) would seem to be spurious. The report by the Kaiser Family Foundation revealed that 'even those who use computers spend substantially less time at the keyboard than they do watching TV' (1999: 24).

The relevance of this for educators is considerable. Children are not gaining access to and not developing skills in the use of ICT for authentic learning tasks, but are mainly using computers for 'fun', often in out-of-school contexts. This occurs at a time when there would seem to be 'a consensus among business leaders, educators, policymakers and parents that our current traditional practices are not delivering the skills our students need to thrive in the twenty-first century (CEO Forum 1999: 6) and it is evident that traditional education environments do not seem to be appropriate for preparing students to function in today's society or to be productive in the workplaces of the twenty-first century.

In early childhood education, there was an initial reluctance to incorporate the use of new technologies, particularly computers, into early childhood programmes. This was basically a result of commentaries which took place in the 1980s (e.g. Barnes and Hill 1983; Cuffaro 1984) which not only regarded the use of the machines as developmentally inappropriate, but also contended that their use was socially isolating at a time in children's lives when social connections were considered to be critical for effective interactions later in life. However, by 1996 there was a recognition by the National Association for the Education of Young Children (NAEYC) that 'technology plays a significant role in aspects of American life today and this role will only increase in the future' (NAEYC 1996: 11). The Association published their policy on the developmentally appropriate use of technology in the early childhood years in response to this growing recognition and called on the profession to 'critically examine the impact of technology on children and [to] be prepared to use technology to benefit children' (p. 11). Seven key issues related to the use of technology in early childhood settings were outlined and discussed in detail. They were:

- the vital role of the teacher in the evaluation of appropriate software;
- the potential benefits of appropriate uses of technology in programmes;
- the integration of technology in early childhood programmes;
- equitable access to technology;
- stereotyping of violence depicted in some applications;
- the role of parents and teachers as advocates;
- the impact of technology for the professional development of teachers.

Inherent to the policy was the notion that ICT should enhance curricula and the recognition that it would not replace traditional activities with materials. Further, the statement defines developmentally appropriate software as being able to:

> engage children in creative play, mastery learning, problem-solving, and conversation. The children control the pacing and the action. They can repeat a process or activity as they like and experiment with variations. They can collaborate in making decisions and share their discoveries and creations. Well designed early childhood software grows in dimension with the child, enabling her to find new challenges as she becomes more proficient.
>
> (NAEYC 1996: 12)

These are indeed worthy goals for any educational resource and should, in fact, be applied to all materials available for use. However, due to the inherent cost of ICT, its use in schools is subject to much more scrutiny. Added to this, in the current educational climate where accountability is measured in test results which do not usually incorporate the use of ICT, the use of computers for enhancing learning is often not an imperative, since outcomes are difficult to measure. Policymakers want to know the *value added* in terms of learning, from expenditure on computers, by asking the question: How do computers improve learning? Yet the question is too simple. We have never asked, How do textbooks, pencils or blackboards improve learning? Perhaps because the cost of these items has never been important enough. It is suggested here that the question we should be asking is a double edged one: In what ways can ICT enhance teaching and learning contexts for *all* children and what are the ramifications of this for curricula in schools?

The role of ICT – a vision for the twenty-first century

In 1995 Negroponte highlighted the ways in which ICT had the potential to revolutionize what we teach in schools. He cited Papert (1980), who focused his ideas on the ways in which computers could provide contexts for learning in which the child was in control of the content and processes of that learning. The model could be epitomized by the phrase 'learning by doing' and was the antithesis of many of the prevailing computer products on the market at the time. This is a critical point, since advocates of computer use in schools present clear arguments about the type of computer activity that they desire, and it does not include 'drill and practice' software, which have limited uses and outcomes in terms of educational criteria. As Negroponte stated:

> In the 1960's, most pioneers in computers and education advocated a crummy drill-and-practice approach, using computers on a one-to-one basis, in a self paced fashion, to teach those same God-awful facts more effectively. Now, with multimedia, we are faced with a number of closet drill-and-practice believers, who think they can colonise the pizazz of a Sega game to squirt a bit more information into the heads of children.
>
> (Negroponte 1995: 198–9)

This model is not learning by doing. There is a need to use ICT in new and dynamic ways and not to perpetuate existing regimes. This was recognized by Clements *et al.* (1993) who noted then that we were at that time at a crossroads in terms of the use of computers in school and trying to decide which path to take (see Figure 6.1). The first path was related to the use of computers as an add-on to traditional classroom work. This incorporated the use of drill and practice software that was

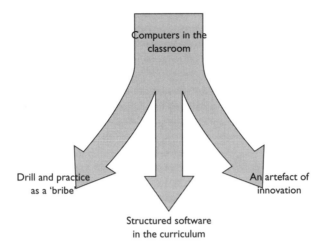

Figure 6.1 Computers in the classroom: which path to take?

generally used to reinforce basic skills, albeit in a technological context, to increase motivation as a reward for completion of regular classroom work. In this way it was often the best students who used the computers or those who were struggling with basic skill acquisition and were deemed to need such specific assistance.

The second path involved the use of structured software in the curriculum. In this category were software applications such as:

- *Electronic books* that could be integrated into a literacy programme as a new media in skill acquisition as well as acting as a catalyst for project work which could be incorporated into the science or social studies curriculum.
- *Sim Town*, which could be incorporated into the social studies curriculum in the context of a study of the nature of settlements and the factors that influence the structures and features that impact on people's daily lives. In using *Sim Town* children are able to design a settlement and invent scenarios to determine the effect that particular variables may have on their town. For example, they may examine the effect of increasing populations on the amount of services needed, or note the effect that reduced water allowances will have on the population.
- *The Logical Journey of the Zoombinis* is an adventure game in which the children design their own characters, called Zoombinis, and send them on a journey to inhabit a new land called Zoombiniville. In doing this they encounter a number of puzzles that they have to solve in order to move their Zoombinis on to the next place. The software has the potential to act as a focus for activities across the curriculum. These may be summarized in the creation of a curriculum web

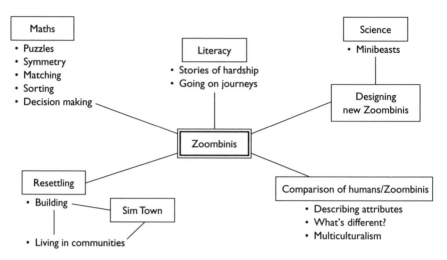

Figure 6.2 Curriculum web: Zoombinis

(see Figure 6.2) and offer opportunities for integration of on- and off-computer work around a central theme.

All of these examples can be construed as being valuable in terms of offering significant learning opportunities, yet they are also examples of the mapping of new technologies on to old curriculum, when in fact what we should be doing is reconceptualizing curricula in schools.

The third path is one in which the computer is used as an artefact of innovation, and implies a reconstruction of existing curricula. Down this path are applications such as the permutations of Logo, derived originally from the work of Papert (e.g. Papert 1980), and may include Microworlds or Geo Logo, and existing open-ended software such as Kid Pix studio, Powerpoint, Hyperstudio and, more recently, applications such as i-movies. The use of such software usually incorporates the integration of other peripherals, such as digital cameras, video cameras, scanners and projectors that of course imply additional costs. In this way the added value of the learning experiences is often mediated by the monetary outlay. The long-term benefits are not as readily apparent in these learning scenarios, even though the short-term evidence in terms of the quality of the overt learning *processes* (collaborative problem-solving and use of higher-order thinking skills) are readily apparent, and the final *products* are usually well beyond that expected by young children. In one classroom I visited recently, children aged 5 and 6 years designed, recorded and processed a video advertisement for the launch of a new product that they had invented. Another group of 7 and 8 year olds in the same school created an animation of a ladybird in action, while their peers created a web page about frogs. This web page not only contained their own carefully researched information complete with digital photographs of local species, but was also linked to other sites designed by schoolchildren or educational professionals. In embarking on these processes the children needed to critically review what was available, make decisions about what to include and debate those that needed to be excluded based on specific criteria.

Environments that have been found to be most conducive for learning are those that reflect the embedded use of ICT across the curriculum. In 2000 I outlined five features of learning contexts that need to be considered when thinking about high quality learning programmes. These are:

- *Learners*: who learn most effectively when they are actively engaged with materials and ideas.
- *Teachers*: who are confident in the use of subject-specific and integrated skills and knowledge, and able to support children's learning.
- *Contexts*: environments for learning which enable children to explore and investigate problems actively and in collaboration with others, using a range of artefacts including ICT.
- *Integration*: recognizing that authentic problems and their solutions require knowledge and skills from a variety of disciplines that can be viewed holistically.
- *Communication*: realizing that sharing the findings of investigations is an important part of learning and a springboard for new investigations.

In this way the use of ICT is incorporated into learning experiences as one of a number of variables, none of which can be considered in isolation. As a consequence they cannot be tested for 'effect' in experimental studies, since they are interactive and interdependent. If they work effectively we have schooling that is characterized by authentic learning in an environment in which all learners, including teachers, are able to gain skills in knowledge acquisition that are relevant and meaningful to them in a variety of contexts. These will include new ways of thinking about literacy and numeracy that are not based in traditional contexts, but within digital worlds.

Ways in which we can enact change in the school context

If we follow the third path, discussed earlier, in which the computer is viewed as an artefact of innovation, our view of the education process could be very different. In various studies (e.g. Yelland 1994a, 1994b, 1995a, 1995b, 1998) I have explored the ways in which young children learn when technology is embedded in a mathematics curriculum called *'Investigations in number, data and space'*. The curriculum is premised on active exploration of concepts with authentic tasks both on and off the

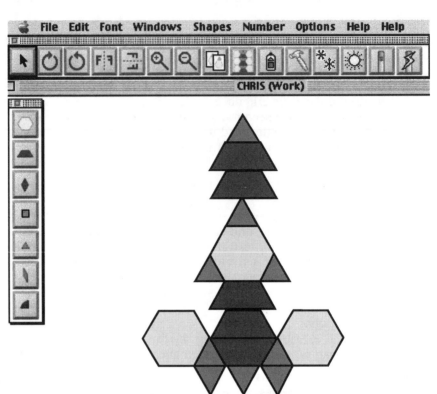

Figure 6.3 Shapes by Chris (6 years)

computer. Computer tasks are both integrated and integral to the conceptual development of each topic. Software called *Shapes* and *Geo Logo*
are included in a number of the teaching modules pertaining to the
concepts of measurement and geometry.

The *Shapes* software is basically two-dimensional representations of
three-dimensional physical pattern blocks that can be played with on
the computer screen. Children are able to create shapes and make
pictures using the on-screen blocks in similar ways to their play with
traditional pattern blocks. An example of a creation completed by children aged 6 years is shown in Figure 6.3. Although the software is based
on three-dimensional pattern blocks there are several differences between
the on-screen version and the wooden blocks. For example, children
can create as many copies of each shape as they want, the shapes can
be combined, frozen (glued), duplicated and arranged to make pictures
on-screen and shapes can be saved and/or printed to make a hard copy
of designs. Clements (1999) has outlined several benefits associated with
these uses that include:

- *Pedagogical benefits* whereby the blocks are experienced in a medium in which they can be stored and retrieved, as well as the fact that they allow children to make constructions that are not possible with physical 'manipulatives'. For example, they enable children to build triangles from different classes beyond the equilateral ones that are provided as part of the set. The children can make non-equilateral triangles by covering equilateral triangles to varying degrees with other shapes, and in doing so create a myriad of triangle types. Further, the printing and storage aspect allows for revisiting and discussing the designs, and they can be taken home or stored in portfolios.
- *Mathematical and/or psychological advantages* in which the on-screen blocks enable children to bring mathematical ideas and processes to a different level of conscious awareness. Such blocks can change the concept of what we mean by 'a manipulative' from being solely three-dimensionally based. They can also allow for the composition and decomposition of shapes and the patterns created with them, facilitating the connection of spatial awareness and number learning.

Evidence supports the notion that the Shapes software can play an important role in children's construction of meaningful ideas in mathematics (e.g. Clements 1999). However, it is apparent that such software cannot do this if it is not embedded in a context that supports the integration of ideas.

Similarly the use of *Geo Logo* is most effective when supported by appropriate scaffolding and opportunities to share strategies with others. Geo Logo is a computer environment in which children direct a turtle using a number of basic commands. For example, the turtle can move forward and back with an input number and make turns left or right as specified by the amount of degrees. As with Shapes, there are on-screen devices that can assist in the creation of and specifications for movements across distances to any given point. Exploration with the Geo Logo tasks has been shown to provide contexts in which children can engage with powerful ideas (e.g. Yelland and Masters 1994; Yelland 1998, 2001) and additionally have enabled them to experience concepts which are well beyond those normally expected for young children. In one example (Yelland 1998) children as young as 8 worked on activities which included the use of negative numbers to 250, quadrants and the development of procedures for action which included the abstract notion of variables, as well as designing projects that incorporated their use (see Figure 6.4). Such concepts are not generally introduced until Year 9 in Australian schools. It is not contended here that the children in the study understood such concepts at the same level as their Year 9 counterparts, but rather that this early exploration with the ideas will fundamentally change the ways in which they think and experience them later, and that this should be accounted for in the curriculum. If this is

Figure 6.4 Year 3 project: TV Man by Alan and David (8 years)

not the case, then the curriculum that they experience will not only be inappropriate, but will also have the effect of alienating students against the subject, which they will deem as boring.

The *Shapes* and *Geo Logo* software embedded in the investigations curriculum demonstrates new ways of teaching and learning with computer technology in the mathematics curriculum that fundamentally challenge traditional content and sequences of subject matter (Clements *et al.* forthcoming). Research associated with the curriculum modules (e.g. Clements *et al.* 1997; Yelland and Masters 1997; Yelland 1998, 2000, 2001; Clements 1999) has not only shown high levels of cognitive activity and the use of higher-order thinking skills, but has also provided case studies of children engaged with learning mathematical concepts in collaborative partnerships, characterized by persistence and interest in the tasks. What is more important is that such research has also demonstrated that the role of the teacher is critical for deep learning of mathematical concepts.

Scaffolding by the teacher together with class discussions about strategies for problem solving have been identified as key elements that promote learning and successful completion of tasks. In this way the computer activity has to be viewed as an integral aspect of mathematical learning and understanding and not as an add-on.

There are many other examples of the ways in which ICT should be integrated into effective classroom practices to bring about change. By creating contexts for learning which are fully integrative and across traditional subject areas we come a step closer to providing authentic experiences for children. Such contexts incorporate skills in literacy and numeracy and afford opportunities to engage with concepts from all curriculum areas so that intersections between subjects are evident. In some cases a topic or theme may be a catalyst for an investigation that requires children to identify a problem or issue, research it, collect and present information and communicate their findings to their peers.

In one Year 2/3 class (7 and 8 years of age) I visited recently, they were studying 'minibeasts' (small animals) as part of their science curriculum. One of the integrative tasks identified involved making a minibeast of their choice, researching information about the particular animal and synthesizing the two into a multimedia production which included an animated sequence of the minibeast coupled with a summary of important information about its characteristics, habitat and other interesting features identified by the children. When the children had made the minibeast they created a backdrop and foreground that represented the habitat of the animal. Thus, if their minibeast was a caterpillar, they created a collage that resembled undergrowth, complete with leaves, twigs and discarded bark. The children then set up a digital camera on a tripod and took a large number of 'shots' of the caterpillar in a sequence of moves that was then coordinated using the i-movie software program on the i-mac. Finally, they incorporated their movie with their information in a Hyperstudio stack so that it became an interactive package which could not only be presented to the class as a summary of their investigation but could also be accessed by others when required. In completing this task in groups of four to six, the children were engaged with processes and content from all the areas of the curriculum, but most particularly from science, social studies, literacy and numeracy. I have completed similar projects with young children using different media such as Kid Pix Studio. In this case the children were 5 years of age and emergent writers, so using an oral medium for the presentation of their 'story' was more appropriate and the use of the slideshow in Kid Pix Studio suited this need. Similarly we could have used Powerpoint for the presentation. New technologies enabled the children to present their information in diverse ways that would not otherwise have been possible and the final products were of such high quality that they exceeded the expectations of work from traditional materials.

Ways of enacting change beyond school

Beyond the school context, there are interesting prototypes being developed in digital worlds. At the Massachusetts Institute of Technology (MIT), digital dolls and toys of tomorrow are being created for playful environments. Researchers in the media laboratory state that their work is based on the premise that:

> The digital revolution will transform the world of toys and play. Old toys will become smarter. New toys will become possible. All toys will become connected. There will be new ways of playing, designing, learning and storytelling ... when a teddy bear sends a hug halfway around the world, when the beads on a child's necklace communicate with one another to make lights sparkle or music sound, we will be playing with the toys of tomorrow.
>
> (MIT 2001)

The researchers at the media lab have created intelligent stuffed toys that can be used in storytelling experiences so that young children can share and save their stories. Umaschi (1998) has also developed another computer-related toy called SAGE that enables children to design their own storytellers to interact with. The toys were designed to let children explore their 'inner world' as well as engage in the storytelling process. The SAGE storyteller is embodied in a stuffed toy with which the children can interact at two levels. At the first level they can listen to stored stories, and at the second level they can create their own stories that can be stored in the toy. Umaschi's work built on the premise that children enjoy interactions and establish relationships with soft toys, and feel at ease in telling them stories.

The use of technology in this context facilitated the interactions, enabling the child to participate in literacy activities that would not otherwise have been possible. Other software such as *My Make Believe Castle* includes digital dolls in a different format. In this application the elements of traditional play are present, including the medieval setting with prince, princess and castle. The digital dolls can be given identities by players and directed to different actions. Papert (1996) contended that digital dolls were more dynamic than traditional ones since actions and personalities are defined by the child rather than at the production level. Again this context provides opportunities for early literacy that are dynamic and interactive.

Where next?

At the present time the rhetoric around educational imperatives seems to be focused on two main issues. The first is related to accountability, which is generally measured in test scores of children's successes or lack of them; the second is related to discussions of 'value added', implying justification for expenditure. Both imperatives have ramifications for the use of ICT in schools. The content of tests tends to be related to traditional subject areas and, because of the sheer number of children involved, they are usually multiple choice in format so that they can be marked electronically. There is little room for lateral thinking or the incorporation of technologically-based tasks. Further, while governments allocate large amounts of funding to place computers and associated peripherals in schools, there are limited funds for the professional development of teachers to ensure that they can learn how best to incorporate the machines into the teaching and learning process. Additionally, the curriculum that teachers are required to deliver often lacks explicit integration of ICT. It may be left to the teacher to make the connection between current offerings of software on the market and the content of their programmes. In such models of curriculum delivery the use of technology in schools is always going to be an add-on to existing experiences.

This chapter has challenged this state of affairs and illustrated ways in which computer-based activities can enhance teaching and learning contexts for all children, specifically those in the early childhood years, and discussed the ramifications of this for curriculum design. It has been suggested that we need to reinvent curricula. Computer activity needs to be not only embedded but also to offer learning opportunities that are authentic, cross traditional subject areas and incorporate the use of ICT as a natural part of the investigative process. Additionally, the use of ICT can enhance the ways in which children share their findings with their peers or community members. In doing this, the forms of presentation of ideas are significantly broadened. The use of ICT also begs a discussion of the role of some traditional activities, such as those described in the introduction, and the inordinate time that may be spent on them.

The use of ICT in schools will not solve all the problems that we face in education today. However, good teachers will have the opportunity to extend their repertoire of good teaching practices with ICT. Examples of exciting learning opportunities for children have been provided here – there are many more stories from other contexts that illustrate new ways that we might be able to engage children in learning in schools. We have an opportunity now to reflect on the ways in which we organize our schools for the twenty-first century. This may mean abandoning some of the old ways and incorporating the new. It is a challenging and exciting time and we should be embracing change rather than perpetuating and propping up tired content, much of which is way past its 'sell by date', just like the qwerty keyboard which was designed to be the most inefficient for typing so as not to jam the 'hammers' together.

References

Alliance for Childhood (2000) *Fool's Gold: A Critical Look at Computers in Childhood.* www.allianceforchildhood.org

Barnes, B.J. and Hill, S. (1983) Should young children work with microcomputers: Logo before Lego? *The Computing Teacher*, May: 11–14.

CEO Forum (1999) *The Power of Digital Learning: Integrating Digital Content.* www.ceoforum.org

Clements, D.H. (1994) The uniqueness of the computer as a learning tool: insights from research and practice, in J.L. Wright and D.D. Shade (eds) *Young children: Active Learners in a Technological Age*, pp. 31–50. Washington: NAEYC.

Clements, D.H. (1999) 'Concrete' manipulatives, concrete ideas, *Contemporary Issues in Early Childhood*, 1(1): 45–60.

Clements, D.H., Nastasi, B.K. and Swaminathan, S. (1993) Young children and computers: crossroads and directions from research, *Young Children*, 48(2): 56–64.

Clements, D.H. and Nastasi, B.K. (1992) Computers and early childhood education, in M. Gettinger, S.N. Elliot and T.R. Kratochwill (eds) *Advances in School Psychology: Preschool and Early Childhood Treatment Directions*, pp. 187–246. Hillside, NJ: Lawrence Erlbaum.

Clements, D.H., Battista, M.T., Swaminathan, S. and McMillen, S. (1997) Students' development of length concepts in a Logo-based unit on geometric paths, *Journal for Research in Mathematics Education*, 28(1): 70–95.

Clements, D.H., Sarama, J., Yelland, N.J. and Glass, B. (forthcoming) Learning and teaching geometry with computers in the elementary and middle school, in K. Heid and G. Blume (eds) *Research on Technology in the Learning and Teaching of Mathematics: Synthesis and Perspectives.* New York: Information Age Publishing, Inc.

Cuffaro, H.M. (1984) Microcomputers in education: why is earlier better? *Teachers College Record*, 85, 559–68.

DETYA (Department of Education Training and Youth Affairs) (2000) *Numeracy, A Priority For All: Challenges for Australian Schools.* Canberra, ACT: DETYA.

Kaiser Family Foundation (1999) *Kids and Media: The New Millennium.* www.kff/content/1999/1535/

MIT (Massachusetts Institute of Technology) (2001) *Media Lab Update.* www.media.mit.edu (accessed 3 Dec. 2001).

NAEYC (National Association for the Education of Young Children) (1996) *Position Statement: Technology and Young Children.* www.naeyc.org/resources/position_statements/pstech98.htm

NCTM (National Council of Teachers of Mathematics) (2000) *Principles and Standards for School Mathematics.* Reston, VA: NCTM.

Negroponte, N. (1995) *Being Digital.* Rydalmere, NSW: Hodder & Stoughton.

Papert, S. (1980) *Mind-storms: Children, Computers, and Powerful Ideas.* Brighton: The Harvester Press.

Papert, S. (1996) *The Connected Family: Bridging the Digital Generation Gap.* Atlanta, GA: Longstreet Press.

Tinker, R. (1999) *New Technology Bumps Into an Old Curriculum: Does the Traditional Course Sequence Need an Overhaul?* www.concord.org./library/1999winter/newtechnology.html

Umaschi, M. (1998) *Soft Toys with Computer Hearts: Building Personal Storytelling Environments*. www.media.mit.edu

Yelland, N.J. (1994a) The strategies and interactions of young children in Logo tasks, *Journal of Computer Assisted Learning*, 10(1): 33–49.

Yelland, N.J. (1994b) A case study of six children learning with Logo, *Gender and Education*, 6(1): 19–33.

Yelland, N.J. (1995a) Logo experiences with young children: describing performance, problem-solving and the social context of learning, *Early Child Development & Care*, 109: 61–74.

Yelland, N.J. (1995b) Mindstorms or storms in a teacup? A review of research with Logo, *Journal of International Research in Science, Mathematics & Technology*, 26(6): 853–69.

Yelland, N.J. (1998) Empowerment and control with technology for young children, *Educational Theory and Practice*, 20(2): 45–55.

Yelland, N.J. (1999) Reconceptualising schooling with technology for the 21st century: images and reflections, in D.D. Shade (ed.) *Information Technology in Childhood Education Annual*, pp. 39–59. Virginia: AACE.

Yelland, N.J. (2000) *The Importance of Effective Numeracy Teaching and Learning in the Early Childhood Years: Issues and Strategies for the Information Age*. Canberra, ACT: DETYA.

Yelland, N.J. (2001) Girls, mathematics and technology, in B. Atweh, H. Forgasz and B. Nebres (eds) *Sociocultural Perspectives of Mathematics Education*. Hillsdale, NJ: Lawrence Erlbaum.

Yelland, N.J. and Masters, J.E. (1994) Innovation in practice: learning in a technological environment, in T. Killen (ed.) *Educational Research: Innovation in Practice*. Proceedings of the Australian Association for Research in Education. http://www.swin.edu.au/AARE/conf94.html (file YELLN94.429).

Yelland, N.J. and Masters, J.E. (1997) Learning mathematics with technology: young children's understanding of paths and measurement, *Mathematics Education Research Journal*, 9(1): 83–99.

Software titles

Clements, D.H. and Sarama, J. (1998) Geo-Logo. Buffalo, NY: University of Buffalo.

Clements, D.H. and Sarama, J. (1998) Shapes. Buffalo, NY: University of Buffalo.

Microworld (1995). Vermont: LCSI.

Sim Town (1998). California: Electronic Arts.

The Logical Journey of the Zoombinis (1996). California: Broderbund.

7

LITERACY AND ICT IN THE PRIMARY CLASSROOM: THE ROLE OF THE TEACHER

Hannah Davies and
Olivia O'Sullivan

The teacher's model of literacy and of pedagogy will drive the electronic writing tools. Good teaching is the most powerful program we can run.

(Zeni 1994: 80)

The discussion and examples of children's literacy experiences with informa-tion and communication technology (ICT) in primary classrooms presented in this chapter arises from Hannah Davies' and Olivia O'Sullivan's work in the Centre for Language in Primary Education (CLPE) in London, UK. They draw upon their interactions with teachers and children, describing the potential of ICT to support and extend meaningful and powerful learning experiences. They also acknowledge some of the difficulties that teachers deal with in implement-ing the use of ICT in current school literacy practices. This chapter outlines an approach to the imaginative integration of ICT into literacy work which requires neither sophisticated technology nor extensive libraries of software. It presents an account of the authors' commitment to the role of the teacher in enabling children to be confident, creative and engaged in their learning for life.

Introduction: the current context: what do we mean by ICT?

It has become something of a truism that ICT is essential to any definition of what it means to be literate in the twenty-first century. In fact, this truism can sometimes obscure the fact that competence with ICT (and by this we mean faxes, videos, computers and computer games) has been an important component of what it means to communicate effectively for the last 30 years. Much ICT is not about some idealized future but a very real part of the present that children are living and learning in. In terms of literacy teaching, ICT can mean a variety of things: use of an overhead projector, a searchable electronic resource, use of a video or imaginative play with a toy cash register in a classroom role-play area. ICT needs to be understood not simply as a checklist of skills to tick off, but as a developing and integrated part of learning in the classroom.

Margaret Mackay's study of a young child, Helen, demonstrates not only the commonplace reality of many different kinds of ICT and competencies that 5-year-old Helen has already acquired at home, but also shows how children live comfortably with multiple versions of texts, linked to different forms of ICT: Helen watches television, can load a video cassette, pause and rewind, listen to music on a tape recorder and play games on a computer using a CD-ROM. Mackay explains:

> Helen also lives in a world of multiple versions of fiction. To take one famous example, she apparently holds a variety of Pooh characters in her head: the Milne-Shepard Pooh of books and pictures, expressed in her parents' voices; the different voices of Pooh on the Alan Bennett tapes; the Disney Pooh as a television cartoon figure and as a paperback book; the Shepard Pooh on her breakfast mug; the Disney Pooh on a T-shirt. Helen seems to live in complete equanimity with all this plurality congregated under a single name.
>
> (Mackay 1994: 9)

Mackay remarks that 'for adults, these different media and different incarnations of fictional characters have a chronology. Books pre-date television, both historically and in our own lives . . . To Helen these distinctions do not exist. She takes this multiplicity of media and versions for granted. Life is just like that' (p. 9). Helen's competencies are replicated in the lives of most children encountered in classrooms in the UK today. Helen's multiple realities present a sharp contrast between the breadth of her experiences of literacy at home, and the 'schooled' version of literacy encountered as soon as she enters the world of the classroom. By constantly seeing ICT as 'new' we may unnecessarily be adding to its mystery and contributing to the fears of some primary teachers that ICT is beyond their grasp, rather than stressing its continuities with more familiar technologies.

In this chapter we hope to avoid these pitfalls. We will not describe high profile projects utilizing the latest technology and expensive extra support. What we want to do is give an overview of how ICT can realistically be used within the *existing* frameworks and curricula, from the beginnings of literacy in the early years through to its role in supporting children to become more confident readers and writers of a whole range of texts. Teachers in England are currently working with a battery of new curriculum initiatives which sometimes present conflicting demands as far as ICT and literacy are concerned. We consider the potential and also the difficulties for teachers in developing the multiple possibilities of ICT in their literacy teaching. We will offer strategies and ways forward by drawing on examples of our own work with teachers and the work of others, in order to show how ICT can be used creatively and confidently, working with but also looking beyond current initiatives.

ICT and the early stages of literacy

For UK children in the early years (ages 3–5) the new Foundation Stage curriculum makes very little explicit reference to the use of ICT (QCA 2000). However, the flexibility of this curriculum, in terms of the views of learning that underpin it, makes it relatively easy for teachers, once they have been provided with resources and relevant expertise, to see the possibilities for including a range of ICT in nurseries and early years settings.

For the most part, it is the implicit opportunities for the use of ICT in the Foundation Stage which are most significant, and identifying these is often down to the enthusiasm and confidence of early years practitioners. For example, in the section of the Foundation Stage curriculum 'Communication, language and literacy', teachers are asked to provide 'opportunities to share and enjoy a wide range of rhymes, music, songs, poetry, stories and non-fiction books'. While there is no implicit inclusion of ICT here, early years teachers have used ICT in the following ways:

- created classroom-made audiotapes of songs and rhymes;
- used living book CD-ROMs;
- used nursery rhyme CD-ROMs;
- created children's own multimedia rhyme book using children's own voices and images (photographs and drawings, both scanned and computer generated);
- used digital still or video images to record and reflect on class experiences (e.g. an assembly or school trip).

In this way, ICT is helping to develop children's knowledge of written language, their confidence in spoken language and their ability in making and communicating meaning within a range of contexts.

Figure 7.1 Nursery children working with a living book

ICT and early reading

One of the ways ICT has been used for a number of years to support early literacy is through the use of living or talking books. Living books are similar in concept to paper texts in that they usually progress from one page to the next in a linear way. They can act as a bridge for young children between the ways conventional paper texts work and the non-linearity of electronic texts such as information CD-ROMs and websites. Living books include animations, a range of sounds, music and opportunities for interaction through clicking on images on screen. The reader is required to navigate their way through the text by clicking on a mouse. Living books such as *Just Grandma and Me*, *The Tortoise and the Hare*, *Arthur's Birthday* and *Green Eggs and Ham* are frequently found in nursery classrooms and allow children to explore such features in a motivating collaborative way. Thus living books offer opportunities for developing both ICT skills and support for early reading.

The following dialogue occurred in a South London nursery class as three 4-year-olds, George, Louise and Elly, were working independently with *The Tortoise and the Hare* (see Figure 7.1). They were familiar with the living book and, as they listened to the text read aloud, their conversation was a mixture of discussion *of* the text and what they would like to activate *in* the text:

Louise: There's that one.
George: That was funny.
Elly [*controlling the mouse*]*:* Shall I do that one?
George/Louise: Yeah.
   All three join in with the song
George: Do that.

Louise: Do that. That's what my brother says. You naughty girl.

George [addressing the hare on screen]: Don't do that again. Go in your house or I'll smack you. Next page please, you do the green one [*points to the forward arrow*], that one, that one . . .

Elly: I've done two [pages]. [*She loses interest now her 'turn' is coming to an end. In a few seconds she moves away from the computer and joins another activity. George and Louise stay put till the end of the story.*]

George [now has the mouse]: Yeah! The race. [*He clicks on the houses on screen, each of which has a song. He and Louise sing along with each house's song.*]

Louise: Do that one again George. [*Meaning click on a house.*] No one comes to the ice-cream man. Press the ice-cream man. The turtle's gonna come . . .

Later on . . .

Louise [now has the mouse]: He's [*the hare*] eating the carrots.

George: Do that, do that that carrot, no I didn't say tomatoes, do that, do that . . .Those flowers are dancing. [*To the hare*] You greedy man!

At the end of the session, George took the mouse, went into the options and credits menus and managed to find his way back to the beginning of the story. In addition he enjoyed playing with two pages in the text where the reader was invited to click on particular words such as 'up', 'down', 'over' and 'water', which were illustrated by animations from the hare and tortoise. George read the word 'water'.

A teacher in a North London Reception class has observed how, even without adult intervention, children using talking book stories had their awareness of the print heightened. All of the children in the class, bar one, made some use of the feature that highlighted the text and read the meanings. Most of the children made particular references to the pages and had a degree of understanding about what they meant in relation to the structure of the story. They were actively using book language such as 'let's turn the page' and making decisions about the contents of the pages, choosing to revisit these in order to retrieve more knowledge, information and enjoyment from them. Even the less experienced children who had previously appeared to find concentrating during story sessions difficult were able to completely immerse themselves in the stories for significant periods of time. This seemed especially beneficial for encouraging and motivating boys with their reading.

Use of a living book can therefore provide opportunities for children to:

* enjoy a text and interact with events and characters on screen;
* read for meaning and enjoy stories with focused talk and joint attention supported by the explicit nature of the text on screen;

- develop their understanding of print through text which is highlighted as it is read;
- develop their own narratives linked to what is happening on screen;
- understand aspects of texts on screen, such as icons, navigational features and 'hotspots';
- develop ICT skills such as use of the mouse;
- collaborate and negotiate with others.

The quality of living books is varied. Some do not invite frequent repetition, and hardly any offer the kinds of support to inexperienced readers which teachers know is vital – elements of rhythm, rhyme and pattern. Myra Barrs has showed how the 'tune on the page' is an important element in supporting young children's reading development (Barrs 1992). While the young children in the South London nursery sang along with the songs within *The Tortoise and the Hare*, the text had few qualities which supported them as readers. Some teachers are also concerned that children may actually be confused by opportunities for clicking on animations, which may actually detract from the narrative.

Julian Grenier, an experienced nursery teacher, has offered the following criteria for evaluating texts:

- Will children get deeply involved in this living book?
- Will the living book encourage two or more children to share attention, talk about what they are doing and collaborate?
- Will children become involved in the story or be distracted by other features?
- Will the CD encourage children to create their own narratives?
- Will the CD encourage an awareness and knowledge of print: does it convey meaning or 1:1 matching of printed and spoken words?

ICT and early writing

The provisional nature of ICT also enables children to experiment and interact with written text. Another nursery teacher in North London observed how, with adult intervention, what often seems like children indiscriminately pressing keys can disguise a more purposeful interaction with language. In this case, the introduction of the word processor encouraged children who were interested in the computer to return to it – asking the teacher to write for them and having a go at producing writing on their own.

Computers and role play

Computers set up in role-play areas, as part of a shop, office, bank or post office can promote explorations both of the computer and of written language. In one literacy session in a London primary school the Reception class divided into groups following a shared writing session.

The classroom included a role-play area, set up as a post office. During this group session in the post office, one child, Tia, chose to sit at the computer. Tia is a bilingual child, who is growing in confidence in English. She decided to type her name:

> 'Where's T, where's T?' [*She finds and types 'T'.*]
> 'Where's I?' [*She finds and types 'I'.*]
> 'Where's A?' [*She finds and types 'A'.*]
> *She presses the space bar*
> 'How do I make it go down?' [*A friend helps her to find the return key.*]
> 'I'm going to make Zoe.' [*Tia looks at the signing-in list in the post office and slowly types Z-O-E, one letter at a time.*]
> 'Now I'm going to make Becky.'

After this, Tia typed a long letter, during which she held her body and fingers exactly like that of an adult touch typist, tapping her fingers over the keys. She produced a page of letters, numbers and other symbols, which she was satisfied with, opting not to print her work. She then decided that the collection of paper, envelopes and stamps on offer in the post office were simply too inviting to resist and joined the other three children who were playing with these. For the classroom assistant observing this group, there was a valuable opportunity to note both Tia's developing knowledge of print through the spelling of her own and others' names, and also how the computer keyboard and print on screen supported this knowledge.

The role of the adult

The role of the adult – either as teacher, parent or nursery nurse – is the key to the use of ICT in developing early literacy. Tina Bruce has characterized the role of the adult in terms of observing, supporting and extending (Bruce 1999). It is only by observing a child working on a computer that one can discern how much learning is taking place. For example, a child who might seem to be randomly pressing letters on a keyboard is actually producing patterns or sequences of letters corresponding to letters in their name. Supporting a child's learning with ICT involves making ongoing assessments and tailoring intervention, including extra help with specific ICT skills such as giving a child some help with using the mouse when the cursor has disappeared from the screen, or helping them to quit a program.

While the children in these examples of early literacy are clearly learning key concepts that underpin literacy and are developing basic ICT skills, central to each of these examples are principles of collaboration, communication, flexibility and the development of children's autonomy by putting them at the centre of the learning. These principles, while more embedded in the philosophy and pedagogy underpinning the

Foundation Stage curriculum, nevertheless offer valuable approaches to the integration of ICT into literacy learning in a more holistic sense across the whole of the primary curriculum. However, as we will go on to discuss, there are greater structural and institutional obstacles within the primary phase of Key Stages 1 and 2, ages 7–11 years.

ICT and the primary literacy curriculum

Reading, far from being an accepted set of traditional operations, is always in need of redescription. Reading needs to be redescribed because the notion that it is an unchanging activity, is, clearly, wrong.

(Meek 1992: 224)

As we have seen in our discussion of living books in the early years, definitions of reading and writing, and the instructional practices that underlie them, are being expanded and redefined by developments in ICT. However, within the primary literacy curriculum at present, definitions of literacy and literacy teaching barely acknowledge this expanding reality. Definitions of literacy and pedagogy have been profoundly influenced by the introduction of the National Literacy Strategy (NLS) into nearly all (state) schools in England in 1999. The Strategy consists of a detailed framework for teaching which extends from Reception to Year 6. Termly teaching objectives are listed under the headings of word level (spelling and phonics), sentence level (grammar and punctuation), and text level (comprehension and composition in writing). It is expected that all or most of the objectives are taught during a given year. In addition, the Strategy puts a considerably greater emphasis on the teaching of phonics, spelling and grammar than existed previously in many primary schools. There is also a greater emphasis on whole-class direct teaching by the teacher. The Literacy Hour has also placed literacy teaching within an intensive daily hour of teaching, broken down into 20–30 minutes of whole-class teaching, 20 minutes of group and independent work and a 10 minute plenary. During this time, the teacher is required to be intensively teaching.

Despite the high priority given to ICT nationally through the UK National Grid for Learning initiatives, this is not reflected in the NLS programme of teaching objectives. There are little more than a dozen references to ICT throughout the hundreds of teaching objectives, and of these, approximately half refer to the use of a spell-checker. The powerful opportunities which ICT offers – for example, for shaping and editing texts on screen, for creating access to information, for communication and presentation of children's work and the creation of new kinds of electronic texts involving multimedia – are present mainly by implication.

Teachers' 'anxious literalism' according to Graham Frater (2000), added to the weight of teaching objectives and time restraints, has meant that many teachers have struggled to see the place of ICT in their literacy and English teaching. At the same time, expectations that teachers should include ICT in their literacy teaching are clearly signalled in another set of curriculum and training documents:

- the National Curriculum for ICT (DfEE 2000);
- the scheme of work for ICT (QCA 1998);
- the funded programme of in-service training for all serving primary teachers (1999 onwards);
- the initial teacher training programme of ICT training.

How are primary teachers to combine the hundreds of objectives and exhortations into a coherent practice in the area of literacy, and include ICT, while working within the tight framework offered by the NLS? At present, the inclusion of ICT in the literacy curriculum presents real challenges and there is a need to develop teacher confidence in, and enthusiasm for, the potential of ICT.

ICT and literacy teaching: establishing a framework for development

Many primary teachers are faced with the problem of knowing what they can actually *do* to integrate ICT into the literacy curriculum. Some teachers simply opt for sticking to what they perceive as being officially required; for others, the issue is solved simply by use of a particular program – to support phonics or spelling for example. Neither of these options offers opportunities to develop the full potential of what ICT can offer within literacy teaching.

The following extract from the Teacher Training Agency (TTA) document for initial teacher training makes a number of clear points about the role of ICT in literacy teaching:

> All primary teachers need to know that ICT has the potential to make a significant contribution to their pupils' learning in English, since it can help pupils to:
>
> - engage with texts in ways which would not be possible through a paper-based activity
> - appreciate the inter-related nature of reading, writing, speaking and listening
> - focus on the content of their writing, at word, sentence and text levels
>
> and that ICT can also:

- enhance basic reading and writing activities
- emphasise the link between the writer and the audience.

(TTA 2000: 4)

However, there are some significant omissions. For example, while there is an emphasis on the editing, checking and formatting capabilities of the word processor, there is little emphasis on the more creative applications of ICT such as multimedia and web publishing, nor on the interactive and information potential of ICT, even within English, let alone literacy across the curriculum.

In developing our courses for teachers at the CLPE we have been supported by a useful framework developed by a group of secondary English teachers and advisers working with the National Council for Educational Technology (NCET, now the British Educational Communications & Technology Agency, BECTA). The NCET framework was developed in order to establish what a pupil's entitlement should be in relation to the secondary English curriculum. What the categories draw attention to are the *processes* involved in working both within literacy and ICT; they offer primary teachers a framework for thinking about how ICT can be used in literacy teaching. We have slightly adapted the categories to fit in with the primary literacy/English curriculum (see Table 7.1).

Table 7.1 A framework for using ICT in primary literacy teaching

Processes, texts and contexts				
Reading texts	*Composing texts*	*Transforming texts*	*Information reading and writing*	*Communicating and presenting texts*
ICT which can support children's reading (e.g. living books) Links between reading and writing Multimedia	Word processing, redrafting, editing Integrating text, images, sounds and animation Creating multimedia Web pages Email	Using existing texts to create new texts or information – manipulating texts and gaining ownership	Extending the range of resources available in the primary classroom Reading CD-ROM and web-based texts Searching for and storing information	Creating multimedia texts Creating web pages Desktop publishing Using email Enhancing sense of audience and purpose
Developing critical literacy and an ability to reflect on own and others' texts				

Source: TTA (2000)

The authors have found that these broad categories provide primary teachers with useful starting points and allow the generation of ideas, instead of restricting teachers to a particular programme or the development of isolated skills. Additionally, an important concept for teachers to consider is that texts encompass much more than print and book-based media – a text can include moving images, animation, sound and images. We have already discussed ways in which ICT supports early reading and writing competencies. As children move through the primary school, the dynamic and interactive properties of ICT can bring real benefits to the composition of a whole range of texts. Composing texts on screen using the unique features of a word-processing or desk-top publishing program rather than simply 'copying out' can provide many opportunities for children to understand texts and how they work. The provisionality of ICT enables text to be more easily manipulated – there's something about writing on screen that feels more practical. Many of the features of a word processor – if used creatively – can serve almost as a hands-on demonstration of how language works.

Contexts

The classroom contexts and opportunities which the teacher creates are also important in the development of pedagogy in relation to word processing and literacy. What word processing can add or develop in relation to children as *producers* of texts, for example, is the facility to:

- compose and change texts with ease;
- take risks;
- integrate different media into a single text;
- extend significantly the range of resources available to the primary classroom;
- create purposeful opportunities for talk and discussion;
- publish and share texts electronically, enhancing notions of communication, audience and purposes;
- use the communicative and publishing powers of ICT to develop notions of form and genre;
- develop critical literacy.

How word processing supports the writing process

Recognition that writing is a process which involves different aspects is recognized by most teachers. The writing process can involve:

- prewriting activities such as thinking, reading, role-play and discussion;
- planning (e.g. listing, drawing);
- composing (e.g. drafting, revising and reviewing);

- editing (e.g. for spelling, grammar, word choice);
- presenting and publishing.

Most of these aspects have been seen as central in all the versions of the English National Curriculum since its inception. While it is possible for ICT to play a role in all of these areas, there are some (such as composing, editing, presenting and publishing) that are more likely to be used than others. The current English National Curriculum, although a shorter, starker document than many of its predecessors, states the requirement for children to revise and edit their work on both paper *and* screen (DfEE 2000). The NLS teaching framework also contains many references to ICT-related tasks, such as 'plan, revise and edit', but because these are linked to particular objectives, the role ICT can play in a child's developing control over different aspects of the writing process is not clearly signalled to teachers.

As adult writers have realized, the processing capabilities of computers offer unique opportunities to writers to plan, shape, revise, edit and present their work. At present, the limitations of ICT resources and time in primary schools mean that in many ways this capability is underused and undervalued by teachers. While children learning to input text (e.g. keyboard skills) is clearly important, this should not become a barrier to using the computer in other ways. Some potential teaching strategies indicated by teachers with whom the authors have worked are:

- In the absence of a whiteboard or visual display unit, use enlarged text on a computer screen to demonstrate to the whole class different aspects of the planning and composing process. For example, make a list of headings on screen, under which could be listed questions for research by different groups of children, events in a narrative or points in writing a report or account. This could then be printed off and used to support writing or research. At the same time, the capability of the word processor in allowing text to be moved and reordered can be demonstrated.
- Discuss a child's text on screen with a group during a guided writing session, or as part of an extended writing session. Issues of structure can be addressed and sections of the text highlighted, copied and pasted or dragged and dropped, as necessary. Issues of style, grammar, word choice and use of standard English can be discussed and word processing skills demonstrated at the same time.
- Headings, side headings and features such as bulleted and numbered lists, fonts and type size can be considered.
- A child's text can be used to jointly proofread a piece of work, looking at ways of using the spell-checker and the thesaurus.
- A variety of ways of publishing and formats can be discussed (e.g. web page, desktop publishing formats etc.).

Once any aspect has been demonstrated, children can work with writing partners on pieces of their work. Children should be reminded at all times to save their work. Saving work to be continued at a later point, together with the opportunity to review what has been written and make changes, is a key feature of using a word processor. All teachers, particularly those who are new to integrating ICT into literacy teaching, agree that using computers in writing takes time and careful planning, particularly when material and time resources are scarce. Sometimes there are real frustrations when computers or printers fail to work. However, teachers agree that the impact of ICT in raising the level of children's writing is potentially enormous. As primary teachers become more confident users of ICT and as the perceived boundaries of the Literacy Hour are relaxed, this area of ICT will become more highly valued by teachers and children alike.

Word processing and poetry: transforming and changing text

Composing large chunks of text is often difficult for children who are unfamiliar with the keyboard and who find it difficult to input text. However, there are many word-processing activities that can be undertaken with smaller units of text. Poetry in particular provides many opportunities for working within Literacy Hour teaching objectives, many of which can be linked to poetry. The NLS website offers some good suggestions (www.standards.dfee.gov.uk/literacy/).

In the following example, a Year 2 teacher in a multilingual school in South London has read several times and discussed with her class a poem called 'The Door' by Miroslav Holub, from *Poems Before and After: Collected English Translations* (Holub 1990).

The Door

Go and open the door
  Maybe outside there's
  a tree, or a wood,
  a garden,
  or a magic city.

Go and open the door.
  Maybe a dog's rummaging.
  Maybe you'll see a face,
or an eye,
or the picture
  of a picture.

Go and open the door . . .

Each child was asked to imagine and then discuss with a writing partner what could be seen through the door. The teacher then provided a writing frame on screen, and, working with a teaching assistant on a suite of four computers in the library, each child, over a period of three weeks, supported by an adult in some cases, produced their own poem, beginning with the same first two lines of 'The Door'. The lines provided a supportive yet open framework. The school did not have access to a scanner, digital camera or the Internet. In this case therefore, the children chose a clipart image to inspire their poem. The teacher felt that the children highly valued their achievement. The results were published in a book which was shared in assembly and showed to parents. Further copies of the book were made for each child to take home. Through this project the teacher observed that using the supportive structure of the poem on a computer enabled many children in her class – particularly those bilingual children at the early stages of English – to reach a higher level of achievement than without the use of ICT. The poems were more sophisticated, children showed greater involvement with the writing process and their self-confidence grew from the publication of their work (see Figures 7.2 and 7.3).

Kanyin

Go and open the door

Maybe outside there's

A flying horse

He will pick me up and carry
me away.

Figure 7.2   Kanyin's poem

Other activities involving word processing and poetry are:

- using the cut and paste or highlight, drag and drop functions to reorder lines or verses of poems;
- writing a piece of descriptive prose and using the highlighter function to identify key phrases and then deleting redundant text in order to create a poem;
- creating 'cloze' activities, based on poems.

Murtaza

Go and open the door
Maybe outside there's
A giant deep hole
Maybe you will fall in it and
get stuck.

Figure 7.3   Murtaza's poem

All of these approaches can be used to create activities which help children to play with the language of poetry, allow them to manipulate text and discuss and change their ideas – in ways that ICT can uniquely offer. In addition, publication of children's poetry in a book, or as a multimedia presentation, can raise the level of achievement even further. All these examples, however, require demonstration, discussion and teacher intervention; as with the early years, many of the learning benefits of these ICT-focused activities come from the opportunity for talk, questioning and higher-order processes. The activities should not, therefore, be seen as a set of isolated tasks to complete.

Information reading and writing

The concept of 'information literacy' is completely bound up with the whole rationale of ICT and the central place it is now being given in the curriculum. The development of digital technologies has led to what many people have called the information age or the information economy, whereby the ability to transmit, understand and sell information and knowledge, rather than material goods and commodities, is what creates wealth – both financial and cultural. The development of digital technologies has led to an explosion of information and information sources using many different media. This explosion creates very real challenges for educators in helping children become confidently literate when dealing with such a range of different information texts.

We have already discussed how ICT can support children's reading development at the earlier stages of learning to read. However, there are bigger issues to consider in terms of reading for information using electronic texts such as CD-ROMs and web pages. We have observed many classrooms where children are asked to go to the computer to find something out about, for example, mini-beasts, using an information CD-ROM. Even in cases where the task is more structured (e.g. how long a caterpillar stays in its cocoon) there is often an assumption that children somehow naturally know how to read or navigate a computer text. Of course, in order to read an information CD-ROM a child needs to be introduced to book-based features such as the contents and index, but also more specific multimedia functions such as a word search facility or using audio and visual cues, such as a loudspeaker icon.

Perhaps the most interesting example of the importance of learning to 'read' ICT is a world wide web browser, where the page displayed on screen contains many levels of information, both text and graphic, some belonging to the web page but also many that are part of the browser itself. On many occasions we have observed children – uncorrected by teachers – typing a web address into the search field of a search engine and completely ignoring the address bar on their browser. As the computer screen with its windows and menus becomes a dominant visual paradigm, learning to 'read' common file menus, recognizing generic icons and familiarity with the look of programs on a screen is an important part of both ICT literacy and literacy in a wider cultural sense. These skills can be introduced to the whole class in a computer suite, or using a centrally placed computer in the classroom, or, alternatively, discussed with groups of children at a time.

From information reading to writing to learn

At the centre of much of the writing about information handling and reading for information is the concept of 'finding things out'. Following on from this we are frequently presented with a set of skills or processes to be followed in order to retrieve the information that the learner supposedly needs to know. In her book *Information and Book Learning*, Margaret Meek argues that the process of reading for information is about much more than simply finding a predetermined piece of information using a set of 'information skills'; reading for information, in her view, is about learning how to learn. She rejects the 'hoop-snake' viewing of learning from information sources as a form of information management based on a positivistic view of knowledge whereby 'the teacher's view of learning and the learner's view of knowing become of less importance than instructions about how the text is to be "tackled"' (Meek 1997: 18).

Meek puts forward an alternative information handling paradigm where the conception of information includes *'uncertainty, probability, hypo-thesis making,* using information in the puzzling-out mode. It starts from the assumption that no information exists as purely detachable fact ... Informative teaching and learning in this mode demand interpersonal dialogue ...' (Meek 1997: 18–19, emphasis added). Meek is, of course, writing explicitly about information books, yet it strikes us that her alternative information paradigm is especially appropriate to approaching electronic information sources and using ICT. Information presented digitally is always contingent, frequently multi-authored, and can be linked dynamically in ways that make finding one definitive answer to an information problem almost impossible. Using ICT, there are always at least three ways of doing the same thing and, indeed, finding the same piece of information.

The explosion of information and information sources that digital media has created clearly requires that confidently literate children learn information handling skills, such as using indexes, searching and checking validity and source. The potential opened up by ICT in terms of how information can be presented, organized and, most importantly, how we can *interact* with it, requires information handling to be seen as something dynamic. Children can learn to see themselves as producers of information as well as consumers of it, where the information they can download can be broken-up, manipulated, re-purposed and transformed into something that represents their learning and knowledge. ICT can also be used to develop strategies, not simply for finding information, but for exploring, manipulating and transforming that information into something meaningful for children. In order for this to happen, teachers too need to understand the dynamic potential of ICT so that activities and tasks related to 'finding things out' make use of the medium in ways similar to the ones we outline below.

The Internet for learning

It may be a truism, but potentially the Internet can bring another world into the primary classroom and increase the amount of information that is available to teachers and students. But the potential of the web is not simply in terms of the amount of information, but of the type and variety that can be accessed, none of which would be available in even the most well-stocked school library. The Internet can make things live and immediate but it can also present a range of different voices and perspectives.

The following sequence of work from a CLPE course, adopted by several teachers, illustrates the pluralistic and dynamic features of ICT in enabling meaningful interaction with digital information sources. Initially, teachers were asked to search for material about child labour during the nineteenth century. As a starting point, they brainstormed information using this framework:

- What do we know?
- What do we want to know?
- How will we find out?

Among a variety of information sources examined were a range of information books, an information CD-ROM of pictures from Victorian times, an encyclopedia on CD-ROM and a website. Teachers found that the website (www.spartacus.schoolnet.co.uk/IRchild.main.htm) was particularly exciting because it included accounts by child factory workers themselves as told to newspapers and parliamentary committees. The teachers and their children were moved by the authentic voices of children and young people speaking to them through the accounts. Sarah Carpenter is one of the many young factory workers listed on the website. Part of her account reads:

> Our common food was oatcake. It was thick and coarse. This oatcake was put into cans. Boiled milk and water was poured into it. This was our breakfast and supper. Our dinner was potato pie with boiled bacon in it, a bit here and a bit there, so thick with fat we could scarce eat it, though we were hungry enough to eat anything. Tea we never saw, nor butter. We had cheese and brown bread once a year. We were only allowed three meals a day though we got up at five in the morning and worked till nine at night . . .

Myra Barrs and Valerie Cork have pointed out that successful writing needs preparation (Barrs and Cork 2001). Pre-writing activities, their research suggests, can raise the level of children's achievement in writing. Use of rich source material such as these young factory workers' accounts therefore suggests a variety of ways of enhancing writing through careful preparation:

- Role-play: using the accounts to enact scenes from children's lives.
- Debates: where the arguments in favour of and against child labour can be rehearsed orally, in role, before being written.
- Comparison tables: used to collect and compare key categories of information from different accounts (e.g. nutrition, conditions of work, ill-treatment). This can be carried out either by highlighting text on downloaded web pages on screen, or by using pens to highlight text on printed web pages.

Outcomes from this work could be:

- Letters written to protest against child labour, using a writing frame constructed with the class, with careful consideration of linguistic and presentation issues.
- A poster, leaflet or newspaper page calling for the abolition of child labour.
- A PowerPoint presentation involving downloaded images and information, with children working in pairs on two or three slides.
- A multimedia presentation using an application such as Hyperstudio in order to share the project with other classes and schools.

Communicating and presenting texts: desktop publishing, web authoring and email

The ability of ICT to combine different media elements makes the move from composition of text to presentation an inspiring and enduring outcome from a unit of work, bringing together a range of literacy and ICT skills. Being able to present professional-looking work is highly motivating for many children, particularly those with special educational needs, and raises the status of their writing. The ability to present text in a range of formats also encourages a very practical understanding of how texts work in a more holistic sense. Asking a child to produce a leaflet promoting a Roman banquet as part of a history topic that stays in an exercise book can seem like a slightly redundant task to the child. Using a desktop publishing program to create headings, insert images and position text on the other hand allows thinking about the purpose and function of a *leaflet* as a promotional tool or as a coherently designed object, as well as just thinking about the individual elements. At the most basic level, inserting a wordart heading or clipart picture can enhance a child's thinking and writing in that they are making choices about what kind of heading best suits the subject, or what an image might make their reader feel.

Similarly, as the work of Tracy Atherton in Chapter 8 shows, children can create their own multimedia to present information in many different forms. As Jane Mitra has pointed out, children are helped to understand how reading multimedia works through becoming multimedia authors themselves (Mitra 1998). In creating multimedia, children need to consider what media are best for presenting a particular type of information – voiceover, graphic or text. This also involves the consideration of audience in a way that is characteristic of higher-order thinking processes. Such an activity also requires the children to talk, collaborate, evaluate their work, draft and redraft, again demonstrating the benefits of a social and collective approach to the use of ICT.

Patty Taverna, a second-grade teacher in Sleepy Hollow, NY in the USA, and Terry Hongell, a computer teacher, have produced a website with children about Harriet Tubman and the Underground Railroad (http:www2.lhric.org/pocantico/tubman/tubman.html). It is an interesting website because of the ways in which children's texts and artwork are used, and also because a variety of ways of presenting information are used: accounts, poems, a timeline and a quiz. This vividly illustrates how ICT allows children to compose and present texts to a high standard, using culturally familiar forms – be it a magazine, poster, multimedia game or website. As soon as an activity is introduced that requires children to present what they have written or found out, they have to think about their audience – few people will read a child's exercise book, but the audience for their work on a website is potentially (if not actually) huge.

Teachers from the early years to Year 6 are finding that use of email as a way of communicating and sharing ideas, projects and book reviews with children in countries all over the world is enhancing the sense of audience and purpose within their classrooms. There are also other ways of utilizing electronic communication technologies such as discussion boards to give children a sense of audience, purpose and excitement in their writing. A Year 6 class in a South London primary school used a discussion board resource on the CLPE OnLine Literacy website which featured opening paragraphs of stories that they then had to continue. The work that they contributed was therefore instantly 'published', raising the profile of their work as well as making them think about the structure and style of the text they were continuing as well as audience and presentation. Some of their comments are reproduced in Figure 7.4.

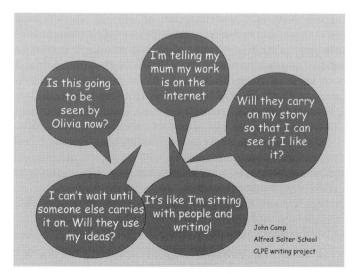

Figure 7.4 Year 6 children's comments

Software and resources

We hope that we have made clear the limitations and possibilities of the real and challenging contexts that teachers are working in. Much of what is achievable can only *be* achieved if adequate resources – both human and technical – are in place. Many resources marketed for primary literacy are designed with specific literacy outcomes in mind and are heavily geared towards meeting predefined literacy objectives, as outlined in the curriculum. In our experience, these kinds of title – although offering potential benefits in terms of motivation or specific remedial help – are not the best examples of how the unique properties of ICT can be best used in language teaching and learning. We feel that it would be useful to provide an overview of the *generic* and *open* software that can perform a wide range of functions and activities and that is widely and cheaply available:

- The most easily available application is a word processor. Simplified versions of standard programs are also available, such as My First Word, which reduces the number of menus and icons available.
- There is also a range of talking word processors which can be helpful for children in the early stages of writing. They can also be good fun to play with, but often the quality of speech is robotic and sounds very obviously computerized. Examples of these are Clicker and Talking Textease.
- There are also many word-processing based software titles that use word banks and/or grids to simplify and speed up the process of 'writing' for very young children or children with special educational needs. Titles such as Clicker contain additional features such as pre-prepared images that can also help reinforce word recognition and can introduce new vocabulary. Teachers can create their own word banks, for example around favourite books, which enable children to create their own versions of these texts.
- Desktop publishing packages abound, from Microsoft Publisher (for older primary children) to Infant Video Toolbox (for younger children). Easybook or Creative Writer offer exciting possibilities with a visual content that appeals to older primary children for creating their own texts.
- Presentation software such as PowerPoint can be used in creative ways which reach far beyond its 'business' formats.
- Multimedia authoring packages such as Hyperstudio and Kidpix (for younger children).

What is important to emphasize here is the generic nature of many of the most useful programs – the key features of ICT that they use are not specific to fancy design or the most up-to-date programming. We feel that a very simple word-processing package is a more powerful tool than an expensive all-singing, all-dancing, narrowly focused 'literacy made easy' CD-ROM.

ICT and literacy: conclusions

The use of ICT in the primary literacy curriculum, in many of the ways we have outlined, requires us to think beyond literacy as a set of static practices for communicating fixed notions of what constitutes correct uses of language. Communicating with ICT requires some conception of visual literacy, of spatial awareness, of sound and of performance. How we communicate is intrinsically bound up with what we communicate *with* – the tools that we use to produce meaning. Writing on a screen is clearly different from writing on paper. But equally, producing a text that includes elements of meaning in the form of buttons or links that the user must select, involves a direct link with the audience quite different from the evocation of atmosphere using a particular adjective.

In an objectives-driven educational culture it is important that we do not lose sight of the big objectives. We must continue to think about what it is that we want children to learn about language and literature and why we want them to learn, and then what are the ICT tools that can help us achieve this. We have outlined ways of thinking about ICT, not just as a useful aid for the teaching and learning of literacy, but as something absolutely central to any definition of a confidently literate future citizen – not simply in terms of skilling children for the information economy but in nurturing their understanding and enjoyment of language, their creativity and their capability for learning for life.

Thanks

With thanks to Mary Fowler, who got us thinking; Julian Grenier, who inspired us to think about the early years; Vivi Lachs and Tracey Atherton, who inspired us with multimedia; and to John Camp.

References

Barrs, M. (1992) The tune on the page, in K. Kimberley, M. Meek and J. Miller (eds) *New Readings*. London: A&C Black.

Barrs, M. and Cork, V. (2001) *The Reader in the Writer*. London: Centre for Language in Primary Education.

Bruce, T. (1999) Unpublished research study for Woodlands Park Nursery.

DfEE (Department for Education and Employment) (2000) *National Curriculum for England and Wales: English EN3: 2*. London: DfEE.

Frater, G. (2000) Observed in practice: English in the National Literacy Strategy, some reflections, *Reading*, 34(3): 107–12.

Holub, M. (1990) *Poems Before and After: Collected English Translations*. Translated by Ian Milner. Newcastle upon Tyne: Bloodaxe Books.

Mackay, M. (1994) The new basics: learning to read in a multimedia world, *English in Education*, 28(2): 29–34.

Meek, M. (1992) Literacy: redescribed reading, in K. Kimberley, M. Meek and J. Miller (eds) *New Readings*. London: A&C Black.

Meek, M. (1997) *Information and Book Learning*. Stroud: Thimble Press.

Mitra, J. (1998) Reading multimedia texts, *Language Matters*, spring: 16–19.

QCA (Qualifications and Curriculum Authority) (1998) *A Scheme of Work for KS1 and 2: Information Technology*. London: DfEE/QCA.

QCA (Qualifications and Curriculum Authority) (2000) *Curriculum Guidance for the Foundation Stage*. London: DfEE/QCA.

TTA (Teacher Training Agency) (2000) *Using Information and Communications Technology to Meet Teaching Objectives in English, Initial Teacher Education*. London: TTA.

Zeni, J. (1994) Literacy, technology and teacher education, in C. Selfe and S. Hilligoss (eds) *Literacy and Computers: The Complications of Teaching and Learning with Technology*. New York: The Modern Language Association of America.

8

DEVELOPING IDEAS WITH MULTIMEDIA IN THE PRIMARY CLASSROOM

Tracy Atherton

'Developing ideas and making things happen' is a strand of the English informa-tion and communication technology (ICT) National Curriculum in which pupils are taught to develop and refine their ideas in a variety of ways. They can organize and manipulate material in different media, create, test and improve sequences of instructions to make things happen and use simulations and models in order to investigate and evaluate changes and patterns in asking the question, 'What would happen if . . . ?' Using ICT to express, explore and evaluate ideas in different forms can be a creative and powerful learning experience. It draws upon the qualities of interactivity, provisionality, speed, capacity and dynamic representation with which ICT can make a distinctive contribution to an activity, supporting higher-order processes of thinking, planning, working and communicating. Tracy Atherton's chapter describes and discusses the ways in which she wove these processes into her work with children in her primary classroom. She identified how multimedia authoring enabled her children to be active in constructing and representing their knowledge with a variety of sources and media, developing their roles as critical and creative authors who were able to evaluate and improve their work for a range of audiences. The processes in which the children were engaged were challenging and high-level, requiring careful preparation, focus and perseverance, honest evaluation and confidence to refine and develop their ideas. The children were deservedly proud of their published presentations which reflected the complexity of the tasks, from critique, planning and

research to organized collaboration and feedback. A key feature of all of this work is Tracy's comment about her role as a teacher. Having framed the purpose and resources of the activity, she had enabled the children to move to a mode of working in which she stated, 'They don't actually need me at all!' This chapter outlines the processes of thinking, preparing, organizing, managing and evaluating which she addressed as a teacher, in order to allow the children to demonstrate what they could do in order to develop their ideas and make things happen.

Introduction: what is multimedia?

The dictionary definition of 'multimedia' is 'the use of a combination of different media of communication; simultaneous presentation of several visual and/or sound entertainments'. Given this definition we can assume that most primary teachers are multimedia experts and that most primary classrooms are multimedia environments, regardless of whether they are equipped with computers. Teachers have, for many years, been using multimedia effectively and creatively to teach. Classrooms have displays using pictures and writing (images and text), and interactive displays where the audience are invited to try things out: which metals will the magnet pick up? Who is hiding under the flap? By simply reading a story with magnetic pictures, using diagrams to illustrate teaching points, using videos, puppets, story and song tapes to motivate, inspire and bring learning to life for pupils, teachers have been employing a range of media without worrying whether or not they are 'multimedia experts'.

Children have been using multimedia to support their learning for as long as teachers have been using it to teach. They have used a range of media to present their work creatively, such as making topic books where they consider content, purpose, layout and design using pictures, writing, photographs, diagrams and moving parts. They have used and created audiotapes to retell stories, interview people, act out plays and record findings. They have used role-play in home corners, re-enacted historical events and performed in plays using sound, speech, action and lighting to both entertain and educate their audience. On top of this, pupils have a wealth of experience of watching television and films where animation and special effects bring the impossible to life. Also, and this is where the pupils have an advantage over many teachers, multimedia games have become household items and the majority of pupils will have at least a passing familiarity with raiding tombs, fighting dragons, solving clues and driving various vehicles very fast in high pressure situations! In other words, they have first-hand experience and confidence in using multimedia and have not only acquired an ability to navigate and interact with it, but also have an imaginative vision of its creative potential. Before we even get to introduce the word 'computer' we can see there isn't much we could begin to tell teachers and their pupils about presenting and communicating with a combination of different media.

However, I wouldn't be writing this chapter if I didn't feel that there was even more to be gained by both teachers and pupils in extending their creative use of multimedia to become multimedia authors. To use multimedia authoring software to combine text, images, sound, animation and video creatively to communicate understanding and to share this understanding with a wider audience is perhaps one of the most rewarding and exciting teaching experiences I have had. I also feel strongly that it is one of the most memorable and educationally empowering learning experiences that my pupils have had. This chapter will describe two projects I set up with a Year 6 class of 10- and 11-year-olds: 'Shakespeare's Tudor London' and 'Rainforests'. It will provide some insight into the process of multimedia authoring, from the management of projects in the classroom to the main points that pupils as authors have to consider. They have to think about a range of issues such as purpose, researching, communicating and presenting content, the target audience, interactivity and being able and willing to evaluate the effectiveness of their work. The chapter is not an in-depth study of multimedia but rather a personal account of my experiences of using it as a classroom teacher and the educational benefits I felt it brought to the pupils and their learning.

Becoming a multimedia author

Imagine walking around a Tudor Maze with tall green hedges and narrow paths when your gaze is pulled to an object lying on the ground. As you bend down to pick up a golden crown you are transported to a meeting with King Henry VII who tells you about himself and his successful battles before sending you back to the maze. You continue walking, passing objects such as drums and stocks and pictures of people pinned on the hedges and every time you get curious and touch one of them, you are played Elizabethan music and shown the instruments, or find yourself in the crowd watching a gory beheading, or are introduced to Catherine of Aragon or Sir Walter Raleigh and told their stories before being returned, again trying to find your way around the maze. And then, as is so typical of mazes, you come to a dead end. There is a loud boom which startles you and you do not know where to go, but on a signpost there is a map of the whole maze, which lets you work out where you are.

(Lachs 2000: 1)

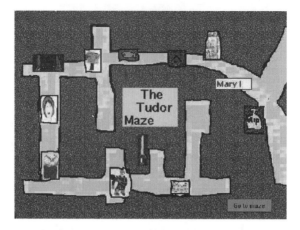

Figure 8.1   The map card from the 'Tudor Maze'

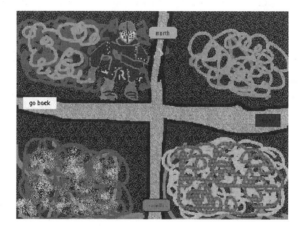

Figure 8.2   A screen from the Maze with directions the audience
need to choose. By clicking on the armour you will link to
a screen of information about Henry VIII

This is a description of the first multimedia project that I was involved
in with a Year 6 class in a Hackney primary school. It is an interactive
multimedia educational game, designed and created by 10- and 11-year-
olds for other 10- and 11-year-olds to use and learn from. I had been
teaching for more years than I care to remember when I was fortunate
enough to have multimedia thrust upon me. I was lucky enough to be
involved in a project working with a consultant who used a multimedia
authoring program for four initial sessions. The result was 'The Tudor
Maze' (see Figures 8.1 and 8.2). Although I considered myself to be fairly

confident and competent in terms of ICT (being the ICT coordinator I at least had to pretend to be!), my use of it in class had been mostly skills based, and in terms of multimedia we had only used word processing with inserted pictures. During the initial planning meetings I found it difficult to have a vision of the end product or of the process itself, as I had never actually seen any multimedia work. Once I did get to look at some examples and saw how the different media could be combined I realized exactly how varied and endless the possibilities were and what an amazing learning tool it could be.

Building a glossary of terms

In order to get to grips with multimedia both the class and myself had to have a firm understanding of certain technological terminology. At first it was quite baffling to us to learn and speak using what felt like alien vocabulary, but it was essential to have the specific and appropriate language to enable pupils to fully communicate their ideas and discuss the creative and practical possibilities of using multimedia. Together we constructed a class glossary of terms that we built up and added to as the project progressed and as new skills and features were learned. This is a selection from the glossary which may prove useful for understanding future references:

- *Animation*: a moving picture created by putting a sequence of different pictures together to show changes or movement.
- *Buttons*: are the means by which hyperlinks are created and other interactive elements such as sound and animation are added to a card. There are basically two kinds of button, visible and invisible. A visible button has a shape and can have instructions, directions, questions or statements on it. An invisible button needs to be drawn around an image or text on the card. When you click on the image it will link to another card, play a sound, show an animation, video or pop up text box (see Figures 8.3 and 8.4).
- *Cards*: the individual screens on which images, text etc. are placed. The cards are like the pages in a book but they don't necessarily follow a linear structure where page 1 leads to page 2 followed by page 3 and so on.
- *Hyperlinks*: the way in which text or images on one card can be linked to text or images on another card. The link is activated by clicking the mouse on the text or image. You can have lots of links going from one card to different cards. These links are not necessarily linear and it is important to remember that the audience will have different choices on where they click and how they navigate the work.
- *Interactivity*: creating ways in which the audience will need to make choices or complete tasks. The user may need to decide where to go next, they may need to choose an answer in a quiz, they may need to drag objects/images around the screen, they may need to find a

Figure 8.3   The Rainforest menu card shows how visible buttons were created to link to the different group stacks

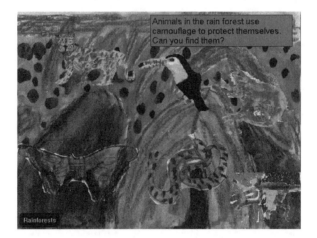

Figure 8.4   The camouflaged animal images are invisible buttons which link to information cards about the different animals and play a sound when clicked. These invisible buttons have been used to create as well as link to other cards

specific object or word. In this way they interact with the information and usually interact with each other.
- *Multimedia*: the combination of different media such as text, images, sound, animation and video.
- *Navigate*: how the user will find their way around the multimedia presentation.
- *Stacks*: a stack is a series of cards that have been linked together. You can also link from one stack to another.

- *Text box*: an area on a card which acts like a word processor and allows you to type in text and change style, colour and size of fonts. You can have a colour background for your text box or you can make it transparent so that the text is on the background of the card.

After being involved in 'The Tudor Maze', my own expectations of what could be achieved with multimedia had grown significantly. I was keen to find out two main things: was it possible to create a more interactive and challenging piece and could I, as a class teacher without external 'expert' support, and with all the pressures of curriculum coverage and timetable restrictions, actually make this happen by myself with a class?

Would-be authors as critics

I have already mentioned that as a teacher I did not have a clear vision of the potential of multimedia until I looked at examples of pupil-authored multimedia work. 'The Tudor Maze' had been designed and created by Year 6 pupils for other upper 10- and 11-year-olds to use and learn from, so that is exactly where I started with my next Year 6 class. We analysed and evaluated the Maze in several ways. First, we played it as a game and considered the following:

- Is it fun?
- Does it hold our attention and motivate us to keep on playing?
- If it does, how does it do this?
- Is it challenging? Does it give us something to do?
- Does it teach us anything? Have we learned anything by using it?
- What did we like best and why?
- What didn't we like or find boring and why?
- How might we improve it?

On the whole, the pupils tried to be discerning and 'professional' in their criticism but they found it difficult to refrain from comparing the Maze with commercially produced games. Just as the actual authors themselves had done, they came up with suggestions that weren't within our power to implement, such as collecting objects along the way to make something happen. However, they did identify some key issues:

- they wanted more to do as the audience;
- they wanted more interaction with the content;
- they wanted to have more control over how they chose to navigate the Maze so they could have more freedom to search for specific items or information.

We then looked at how informative the Maze was and how easy it was to find out about the Tudors by using it. The conclusion was that there was a lot of quite interesting 'stuff' but it wasn't really part of the game and so the pupils didn't pay much attention to it and therefore didn't remember much about it. They also complained that they got stuck in the Maze and could only find things by chance. This, they felt, was very frustrating and meant they couldn't use the Maze as a source of information. Of course there is no greater critical audience than your peer group, and my class of 30 10- and 11-year-olds were already convinced they could and would do better than the last lot before they even laid eyes on the Maze, so they weren't the gentlest of critics.

Finally we analysed the structure and design of the Maze by mapping out how the different cards were linked together and what areas of information had been covered. This was no easy feat and the pupils revised their rather harsh judgements as they realized just how extensive and complicated the Maze was and how much planning and organization the previous class would have had to do in order to create it. In the end, in spite of themselves they had to admit they were impressed . . . but not completely overawed!

Their scrutiny of the work had three important effects. First, it gave the pupils an awareness of the creative potential of multimedia: of how to use images, sound, text and animation effectively. This meant that we were able to take into account one of the most important aspects of multimedia authoring: how to combine media and how to make decisions about what are the most effective and appropriate media to use when presenting specific pieces of information. One of the dangers in multimedia authoring is that features of the software dominate and dictate the content. For example, after being shown how to make 'dragable' images, one particular group became obsessed with this feature and tried to make their content and presentation include 'dragable' images on every card. This defeats the whole purpose of a project. If need be, ban it, as I did with this group which forced them to think about the best way to present rather than allowing themselves to get carried away with special features. In a more appropriate example, the 'Tudor Street' group made the decision to use animation on their cards because they felt it was the best way to explain their information to a peer group audience (see Figure 8.11, p. 140). By doing this they eliminated the need for a lengthy textual explanation as well as entertaining their audience and bringing a feature of Tudor history to life. The only text needed was a brief explanation about a specific feature of Tudor architecture. The only aspect they couldn't recreate was smell! So they incorporated sound to inform their audience about this.

Second, it fired their imaginations and motivation. They needed no further encouragement from me to take on the problem-solving task of designing and creating a multimedia presentation for the purpose of teaching their own peer group. The only real difficulty was in restricting their imaginations within the bounds of what was actually possible given the software limitations.

Finally, it also produced an understanding of the importance of audience. When creating their own work, they knew that it in turn would be used, admired and criticized by other pupils and that it would have to stand up for itself – they would not be there to explain and defend it.

Starting the projects

Setting the scene

We are in an Inner London Hackney primary school with 30 Year 6 pupils in the autumn term. Among the 30 there are 2 children with full special needs statements, a further 9 on the Special Educational Needs Register and 23 out of the 30 speak a language other than English. We have one computer, six portable word processors, a scanner, a digital camera, a whole lot of enthusiasm and a stack of imaginative and creative ideas for our multimedia project. How do we get organized?

Planning and classroom management

Our history topic on the Tudors was given a focus by a visit to the Globe Theatre, and our Literacy Hour work on Shakespeare gave us a chance to show off our growing and very grown-up knowledge of Shakespearian plays and theatre. The class as a whole decided to base their Tudor multimedia presentation on 'Shakespeare's Tudor London'. First we brainstormed our ideas to decide what areas we would need to cover (see Figure 8.5).

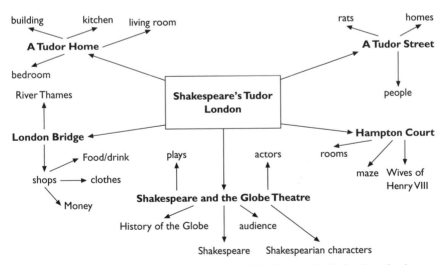

Figure 8.5 The 'brainstorm' plan for 'Shakespeare's Tudor London'

We had already decided collectively that we would be making our piece for other upper Key Stage 2 pupils who would be learning about the Tudors and that this would dictate what information we put into it. We had to think about how we were going to present this information, how we would hold our audience's interest and challenge them and, of course, how much we would impress them with our boundless knowledge, creative artwork and advanced ICT skills.

I split the class into five groups of six so that each group had responsibility for one area. These groups were mixed ability and would be working together during ICT sessions, some art lessons and some history sessions. Other work would go on during the Literacy Hour, but then the pupils would be working in their literacy groups at their own level. As a whole class we then had some discussion about the main points we would need to consider in our groups when planning our work. This was the initial checklist we devised:

• what information we needed to research and where we would find it;
• what images we needed to create;
• how many cards our group stacks would have and how they would link together;
• how we would make the piece interactive;
• how to divide the work up within the group.

We also at this point created some group working rules to ensure that all group members participated fully, that all contributions would be valued and different strengths utilized fully and appreciated. The class were used to working in groups but often worked independently within a group. This total collaboration brought a new set of challenges for the pupils and was one of the great learning benefits of the project.

The groups then collaborated to come up with a group stack plan so they could then take on the task of designing the individual cards.

The Globe Theatre group produced the plan shown in Figure 8.6 showing how all their cards would link together through a menu card. The bold initials are the children who were to have responsibility for that particular card. The group decided together that they would do some of the cards in pairs and others individually and that they would report back to the group as a whole for feedback and reviews of the work as it progressed. During this process of course the 'natural born leaders' of the groups emerged. In this particular group the 'leader' was elected unofficially by the other members. 'Ibrahim will be in charge of checking that we're all doing what we should be doing,' Mehmet reported to me, 'because he's good at sorting things and we don't mind being bossed by him 'cos it doesn't sound like bossing when he does it.'

The groups then worked individually or in pairs to design their screens or cards. They were given a template that covered the main points they

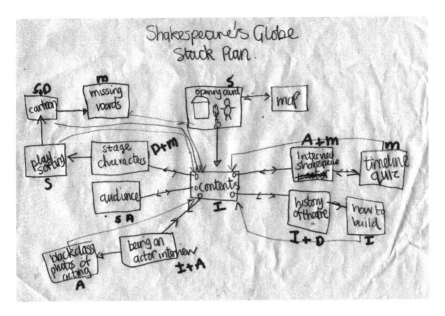

Figure 8.6 The stack plan for the Globe Theatre group

would have to consider in the design and space for sketching out in rough how they wanted their card to look (see Figures 8.7 and 8.8).

Femi and Zerlina, the designers of the cards shown in Figures 8.7 and 8.8 had to think not only about the content and presentation of their cards but also how their cards linked to the whole stack and how they were going to combine different media to communicate their information and to create interactive elements for their audience. Femi, who was a bit of a mathematician, wanted to provide some maths content in his card on Tudor vintners. He created different sized wine bottles and capacity labels to provide an interactive 'drag and match' activity around capacity.

In terms of planning as a teacher I had to consider where the multimedia authoring fits into the curriculum, how and when were the pupils to be taught the history they needed to cover, how and when were the pupils to be taught the ICT skills and software knowledge they needed to cover and how and when they would research and create the content. The following is a rough indication of time allocation and organization for this:

- Two 30-minute sessions a week on teaching and reviewing ICT skills. During this time I might introduce a new feature of the software – for example, making objects 'dragable'. I would model how to do it, then one of the pupils would demonstrate how they could make an object on one of their screens dragable, giving explanations of what they were doing as they went through the process. We might also review

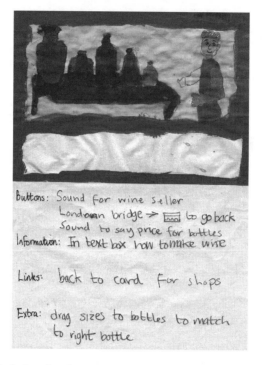

Figure 8.7 A design for the vintners card, part of the London Bridge group.
The final piece of artwork has been pasted over the original rough sketch

previously introduced skills such as scanning images, resizing or copying and pasting images, by getting other pupils to demonstrate the
skills needed but using work that was part of the ongoing project.

- One afternoon a week was devoted to covering the history curriculum,
  but during this time research of information would also take place and
  pupils would often be using the computer to find information or using
  portable word processors to create text needed.
- We had a weekly one-hour art session that was sometimes linked into
  the project – for example, Tudor portraits, models of Tudor homes,
  Tudor costume designs etc.
- One afternoon a week was set aside for project work when the groups
  would come together to create their screens and prepare content.

Often during this time it felt like multimedia madness. One group
would be putting on Tudor clothes and taking photographs with a digital camera. Another group would be creating an animation of a Tudor
street where someone is emptying the 'waste' by throwing it from the
window of a Tudor home. Yet another group would be role-playing an
interview with Shakespeare in preparation for recording it on to their

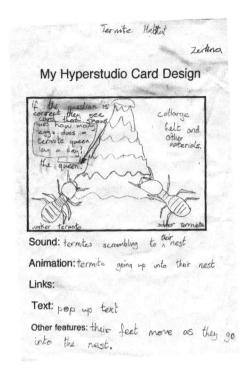

Figure 8.8 A card design from the Rainforest project which shows the original rough sketch for one of the termite cards from the Creepy Crawlies group

screen later. Several pupils would be using portable word processors and researching information. A few more would have printouts of their screens so far and be going through their plans, reviewing the work completed. One pupil would be showing two others how to make pop-up text boxes on a screen. A final group would be creating the artwork needed for their screens. I would sometimes be going from one group to another to offer support or focusing on a particular group who were trying to overcome problems or use a feature of the software for the first time. As the project progressed I often found myself standing in the middle of this busy, multimedia classroom thinking, 'They don't actually need me at all.'

At the end of these sessions we always made time for a project plenary when a particular group would share the work they had done with the rest of the class, explain the processes they had gone through, highlight any difficulties and point out the bits they were particularly pleased with. The class would then respond with feedback, offering suggestions for improvement and praise for the work shown. As you can see from this description, a lot of the work for a project of this kind actually takes place away from the computer; the computer is just another tool to be used when necessary and to bring all the work together. Initially a lot of the pupils found this quite hard – they absolutely *had* to be at the computer, but gradually this need diminished as they realized for themselves that all the work was part of the ICT and that the computer was useless without any of the other work being done. This basic approach to the project and the classroom organization of it was used for both the 'Shakespeare's Tudor London' project and the 'Rainforests' project, although there were some key differences in terms of what the class had to consider in relation to purpose, audience and interactivity.

Audience

The awareness of audience is quite a difficult concept for children to grasp. Given that their usual audience at school is the teacher and other members of their class who are a physical reality, it is a leap of faith for them to have to consider the needs of an audience who they will never see or speak to. It is somewhat easier for them to target a peer group audience on a wider scale when first producing multimedia. At least they have a more 'real' insight into the needs, likes and dislikes of their own peer group by thinking about what they themselves respond to. 'Shakespeare's Tudor London' was created with Year 5 and 6 pupils in mind, but for the later project on 'Rainforests' the class were given the more difficult task of designing and creating an interactive multimedia presentation to be used by younger Year 2 and 3 children as a curriculum resource. This difference in audience had a major impact on what the authors considered to be important in the designing of their screens and the planning of the whole project.

Multimedia for a peer group audience

When designing for a peer group audience the class came up with the following:

- *The piece needs to look good. We want to impress other 10/11-year-olds with our artistic skill* (see Figure 8.9).
- *Don't put them off with too much text. Use other media to explain and inform, or 'hide' the text in some way* (see Figure 8.10).
- *Grab their attention by entertaining as well as informing. Humour is important* (see Figure 8.11).
- *Hold their attention by challenging them. Set them tasks to do but make it like a game* (see Figure 8.12).
- *Make sure they really pay attention by forcing them to engage with the content by creating interactive elements.* An example from the Globe stack illustrates such dual interactivity. The user clicks on any of five

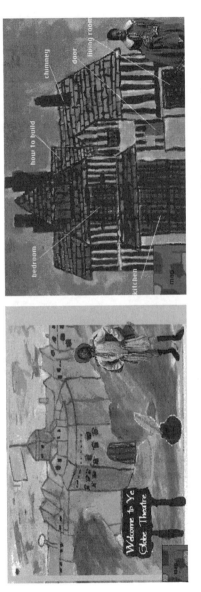

Figures 8.9 Screens from the Tudor project using painted backgrounds and digital camera images of pupils in Tudor costume

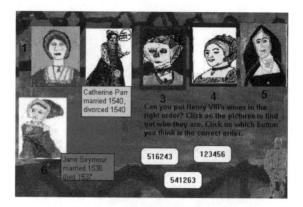

Figure 8.10 A screen showing portraits of Henry VIII's wives hanging in Hampton Court. By clicking on the pictures you see a pop-up text box that gives information about the different wives. You then have to select the button that shows the correct order in which the wives were married to Henry VIII and if you are correct you will be rewarded!

Figure 8.11 The Tudor street where you may have something nasty thrown over you! By clicking on the animation button the audience actually get to see what might have happened on a Tudor street complete with sound effects to let you know how smelly it would have been too!

Shakespearian characters to hear them speak a line from the relevant play or to see the quote appear in a pop-up text box. They then match the name of the character to the correct image by dragging and dropping name labels. A further example is the 'Tudor Clothes Quiz' where the user reads several 'Amazing Tudor Fashion Facts' and clicks a button to say whether they believe each fact to be true or false.

Figure 8.12 On these two screens the images speak when clicked to set the challenge. Henry VIII tells you to find the Tudor crown jewels by completing the tasks on the other cards. The shopkeeper gives you an amount of money to spend so you need to find the right shops on London Bridge

The example screens shown above go some way to demonstrate how well the class considered the needs of their audience, but in true multimedia style a printed screen is not sufficient to demonstrate the effects and impact of sound and animation. It is also clear how intrinsic the awareness of audience is to the other considerations of purpose and interactivity. This became even more apparent during the second project on 'Rainforests'.

Multimedia authoring for a different audience

During the summer term we embarked on our second multimedia project. By this time the class considered themselves to be multimedia experts. The challenge had to come from having to consider a different set of needs and expectations of a less familiar target audience. As a class we were involved on a topic around 'Rainforests' so we decided to create a multimedia piece aimed at Year 2 and 3 pupils and use the rainforest topic as a means of teaching these year groups about plants, animals, minibeasts and insects.

When designing for a younger audience the class came up with the following points to consider:

- *Make it easy for them to understand by using clear images and easy to read fonts.* The opening card created by the group dealing with plants had clear pictures of the parts of a flowering plant, and easy to read labels for each part, which say the word when clicked. Simple, clear instructions guide the user to drag and drop the pictures to make a whole plant, and then label it. 'Clear' does not necessarily mean less detailed or informative. For example, the card produced by the group dealing with insects to explain termites had images of a queen, soldier and worker termite, each clearly showing their individual characteristics. (It is interesting to note that the class on the whole were less concerned about impressing a younger age group with stunning artwork. Although they still wanted it to look good they presumed that your average 7-year-old would be sufficiently impressed by an average 11-year-old's artwork! However they did acknowledge that even 7-year-olds would like a little visual variety.)
- *Use a range of visual images to hold their attention and bring the subject to life* (see Figure 8.13).
- *Combine the media to reduce the amount of text used: 7-year-olds will be even less inclined to read lots of text than 11-year-olds!* This was effectively achieved by the plants group who created a card to show and explain the life cycle of a tree. They used six scanned images of the various stages of growth which, when clicked, gave voiceover explanations of what was happening in the picture. The images were numbered and had to be dragged into their correct order and then correctly labelled.

Figure 8.13 A close-up digital photograph of a rainforest model. When clicked it takes the user on a tour through the rainforest to view the model from different angles. Other cards used scanned images of embroidered felt collage scenes showing the animal life and vegetation in the forest, and a computer-drawn globe revolves to show areas of rainforest around the world

The correct sequence could then be checked by clicking a button. If right, the user is transported to a second card which shows the growth of a tree. The two cards successfully combined images, sound and animation to teach and test the user without overwhelming them with lengthy textual explanations.

- *Listen to our audience, they know what they like. Get feedback from the target audience so we can review the work as we go along.*
- Remember the purpose of the work. Make sure we teach our audience what they need to learn. But how do we know if they've learned something?

At regular intervals throughout the project we invited 'guinea-pig' pupils from the Year 3 class to test our work. They used the piece in pairs and then the class would ask for their comments and question them to get appropriate feedback. In spite of some of the Year 3 pupils being a little in awe of Year 6, they were quite forthright in their criticism. After using the tree life cycle card, Daniel told them, 'I can't be bothered to read all them words [he meant the labels] so I can't do the game bit.' Samuel, who was in the process of creating two cards to teach the pupils about the life cycle of a caterpillar, took this statement very much to heart, then went away and produced a card which showed an animation sequence of the caterpillar hatching from an egg through to the butterfly emerging from a cocoon: *The Very Hungry Caterpillar* in four seconds! There was no text other than the title and all other information was given as a voiceover sound recording. He then created a second card with a drag and drop game on it, again using sound rather than text. He had scanned in four painted images showing egg, caterpillar, cocoon and butterfly. The user had to drag the images into the correct order. Daniel approved wholeheartedly when he came to 'test' the work and he was able to describe and explain in detail what he had learned about the life cycle of a caterpillar, without having to read at all!

The only thing that still concerned Samuel was that he had no way of checking that the user had dragged the images into the correct order. But he provided the Year 3 teacher with a fairly reasonable assessment solution: 'Just get them to do it and then they can print it and see if they can write on the work about the different bits. Then you will know if they understand or not.' I feel Samuel may have a future career in teaching if he doesn't take up multimedia design!

The last point in the list, about knowing the audience has learned from the software, raised a lot of interesting discussion. The class saw themselves far more clearly in the role of educators when designing for a younger audience. They felt a responsibility towards their audience and began to take on the worries and anxieties that an average teacher suffers on a daily basis. Are the pupils paying attention, have we made it interesting enough, have we allowed them to practise enough, have we checked that they have understood? The children were constantly asking themselves such questions.

Ayshe and Daryl commented, 'We have to do what you do Tracy. Like when you teach us some new maths, we practise it like a game and then we remember it better. Then you give us a test or something to check we know. When we work at it and get it right then we get a reward.' This statement makes me sound like a cross between a Victorian schoolmistress and a dog trainer, but they had got the right idea. Children need incentives and encouragement to learn and teachers (themselves in this instance) need to provide them in terms of interesting and memorable teaching and activities and acknowledgement of their efforts and achievements.

This led to what can be described as a 'Teach, Test, Reward' structure to some of the group stacks. On the tree life cycle card tested by Daniel, the user had to select the button that showed the correct sequence of the life cycle. If they got it right they would be rewarded with an animation of the tree growing from a seed. On the bee section of the insect stack, Ayshe asked: 'Where does honey come from?' She then gave three choices: flowers, bees or flies. Clicking the correct answer resulted in a reward in the form of an animated bee flying from flower to hive.

The class was forced to consider the needs of their audience in a far more deliberate and thoughtful way than they did on the first project. They also had to allow for, and respond to, user feedback which came from a sample of that audience rather than simply evaluating the work themselves. This required a very mature and collaborative approach and made them analyse the work more critically to ensure its effectiveness.

What did we learn?

A lot of my own assessment of the work and the achievements of the pupils was cross-curricular. For the first project the pupils exceeded the learning objectives set out by the history National Curriculum. Having to 'teach' others about the subject meant they certainly had to learn more. The class would discuss features of Tudor history as knowledgeably and enthusiastically as they did Pokémon cards, soap operas and pop groups. It had become part of their 'culture' and gained a status that schoolwork usually lacks. They also developed literacy skills throughout the work, especially in writing for a specific purpose and audience. In terms of their ICT skills and knowledge, and how confidently and independently they applied them, they were working at a level beyond National Curriculum expectations. An Office for Standards in Education (Ofsted) inspector who observed a lesson commented that he had never actually witnessed Year 6 pupils achieving 'Level 4' out of the 63 inspections he had been involved with, and he assessed some of the class as working at 'Level 5' with regard to how they considered audience in their work. Pupils with special educational needs progressed dramatically, not only in academic terms but in terms of self-esteem and behaviour. For me, the greatest benefits were to be had in the aspects of children's learning that aren't measured in National Curriculum levels: creativity, collaboration, cooperation, autonomy, self-motivation, self-assessment and simple enjoyment of learning. Multimedia authoring brought learning to life for all these pupils. It gave them an opportunity to be active learners and educators in a way they had never previously experienced.

It is not necessary to carry out projects of this size to reap the benefits of multimedia authoring, and neither is it the domain of Key Stage 2 pupils only. Creating mini 'living books' with talking characters, making a 'talking heads' class project on ourselves, designing an interactive maths game to teach younger children about number bonds, animating a favourite poem or rhyme or producing an interactive guide to your school are all possible with multimedia, and teachers have been providing pupils with the skills and opportunities to do such things for years. Now we can do it with computer technology. The computer is there to extend the imaginations and expectations of both pupils and teachers. It is not about hard drives, broadband connectivity, megabytes and peripherals. It is about utilizing a teaching and learning tool to its full educational and creative potential. Let's make the most of it.

Reference

Lachs, V. (2000) *Making Multimedia in the Classroom: A Teachers' Guide*. London: Routledge Falmer.

9

CREATING AN ONLINE PROFESSIONAL COMMUNITY

Babs Dore

Chapters 9 and 10 look at the development of teachers' personal and professional information and communication technology (ICT) capability by focusing on UK students training to teach in the primary school on a one-year course for the Postgraduate Certificate in Education (PGCE). This chapter considers the use of an online asynchronous discussion forum to extend opportunities for students to share issues arising from a challenging course. In Chapter 10 the student teachers demonstrate their growing understanding of appropriate use of ICT in their professional development. Computer mediated communication (CMC) here refers to the use of an asynchronous forum, one in which messages can be accessed via the Internet at any time and discussion is threaded under a topic heading. Nationally the use of such networks is a way of 'supporting professional debate about professional issues' (Leask 2001: 6) and is referred to in the ICT standards within the Initial Teacher Training National Curriculum. There is debate as to the efficacy of such networks, particularly those that exist on government sponsored sites (Leask 2001). Nevertheless, a growing number of such discussion facilities exist informally (either as asynchronous forums or email lists) and provide a mechanism for the exchange of information or the sharing of resources.

Introduction: professional development in ICT in primary schools

The appropriate use of ICT in education throughout the UK has been much under scrutiny in recent years. Within Initial Teacher Education this has resulted in the inclusion of specific standards for the use of ICT in subject teaching in the Initial Teacher Training National Curriculum (DfEE 1998). Serving teachers are also now expected to demonstrate these same standards as 'expected outcomes' after a course of in-service training funded from the UK National Lottery through its New Opportunities Fund. Most of the training offered to serving teachers has been via the medium of ICT itself rather than more traditional face to face training methods. Indeed most of the materials are CD-ROM based and support is typically provided through tutor-supported online discussion. Similarly, working within an already packed timetable, teacher trainers have had to find ways to accommodate a much expanded requirement to develop student's own ICT capability in both a personal and professional context. In many institutions the solution has been to support conventional face to face ICT sessions with an online asynchronous discussion forum and the increasing provision of online materials.

Teachers and students need time to develop and reflect upon their understanding and confidence in the appropriate use of ICT in their classrooms. In a demanding one-year course, the opportunities for practice and evaluation by students and teachers are pressured and constrained by time. Furthermore the imperative expressed by the students at this stage is on 'knowing what' and 'knowing how' rather than 'knowing why'. However, students and teachers embarking upon new initiatives can benefit from a forum in which more reflective discussion can take place. Earlier work in projects using an asynchronous forum with distance learning students suggested that this was an appropriate medium through which to encourage students to 'explore issues, take positions and evaluate their own perspectives' (McLoughlin and Oliver 1999: 36). This chapter presents a discussion of the contribution of computer mediated communication (CMC) to creating an online professional community, focusing on the experiences of primary PGCE student teachers at the University of Brighton to illustrate their processes of practice, reflection and shared discussion.

Issues in the use of CMC

Supporting reflective learning

Kolb (1984) sees the learner as an active participant in the construction of knowledge through experience and reflection on experience, highlighting the dynamic relationship between 'knowing why' and 'knowing how'. Such learning is 'realised through interaction and dialogue in social contexts' (McLoughlin and Oliver 1999: 35). Participation in an online forum offers a unique medium for facilitating deeper levels of understanding through conversation, argument, debate and discussion. On the PGCE course, CMC offered the opportunity to initiate a 'learning conversation' outside the restricted timetable. The forum provided an accessible medium within which students could 'go beyond their experience, [to] use it and reflect on it and thereby change their perspective on it, and therefore change the way they experience the world' (Laurillard 1993: 26).

Within the context of Initial Teacher Education, students need to be given encouragement and opportunities to begin to construct a personal pedagogy from the elements of their course (Selinger and Pearson 1999). Teachers themselves find it difficult to articulate what they do that is successful in the classroom, recognizing that much of their expertise is situated in context and built up over years of experience. How then were beginning teachers to acquire the insights that would enable them, so early in their course, to plan for effective use of ICT in their teaching? They needed a means by which they could link theory and limited experience and begin to frame an understanding of the 'distinctive contribution [which] ICT might bring to a learning situation and know when and how to use digital technologies appropriately' (Loveless *et al.* 2001: 67). Ideally, in a traditional face to face course a forum exists for facilitating these discussions, either formally in tutor-led seminars or in informal opportunistic exchanges, when experiences are shared and knowledge of the craft constructed.

Diana Laurillard (1993: 168) highlights the benefits of student to student discussion in enabling students to find out what they do and do not know, but emphasizes that the 'pedagogical benefits of the medium rest entirely on how successfully it maintains a fruitful dialogue between tutors and students, or indeed between fellow students'. Within an online discussion forum students can be encouraged towards critical reflection, examining practice by articulating it – a 'public presentation of thoughts' (Selinger and Pearson 1999: 22). Having to make explicit one's own knowledge and understanding to others via the forum can help to formalize personal understanding. What's more, the community of learners could be extended to include experts (tutors or serving teachers) outside of the institutional setting and the discussion could be supported over time.

This model of CMC-supported learning sees the tutor acting as scaffolder to transform the group experience into the construction of knowledge by structuring and supporting the process of discussion. The tutor/ mediator holds a pivotal role in establishing and maintaining such a conversational framework, and while the medium offers opportunities for reflection on participants' contributions, its success is totally dependent on good moderation by the tutor. Salmon (2000: 39) describes the e-moderator's role as 'engag[ing] the participants so that the knowledge they construct is usable in new and different situations'. This evolution in thinking and action within developing online discussion is modelled by Salmon (2000: 25) into five stages:

- Stage 1: individual access and the ability to use CMC.
- Stage 2: establishing individual online identities and finding others with whom to interact.
- Stage 3: exchange of information relevant to the course.
- Stage 4: course-related group discussion – interaction becomes more collaborative, communication depends on the establishment of common understanding.
- Stage 5: participants explore how to integrate CMC into other forms of learning and reflect upon the learning process – a constructivist approach to learning.

Encouraging active participation

From previous experience in the use of an asynchronous forum, we had identified a number of common themes that emerged in relation to the development, implementation and maintenance of successful discussion forums. These fall into four main categories:

- problems with initial access that inhibit take-up; student lack of familiarity with the system; the need for technical support;
- barriers to communication online; lack of group identity; lurking; anxiety; posting to a permanent, public forum; student expectations;
- the need for tutors to become active mediators; implications for staff development and tutor time;
- pedagogical issues arising in facilitating discussion; lack of context cues; encouraging the move from description to analysis, from social interaction to reflective discourse.

Problems in initiating and sustaining an online discussion are well recognized in the literature when, despite tutor mediation and encouragement, the participation figures for those conferences where contributing is not mandatory seem to hover around the 25 per cent to 30 per cent mark (Edwards and Hammond 1998; Jones *et al.* 1999; Stratfold 1999).

Student skills, needs and interests play an enormous role in determining initial take-up on the forum, but it is also essential to recognize the need for time to become familiar with this new form of communication. Salmon (2000: 27) stresses that students need 'information and technical support to get online, and strong motivation and encouragement to put in the necessary time and effort'. They also need to be assured that, once technical problems are overcome, it is the 'use of the technology by people that makes it ... ultimately a learning experience' (Nixon and Salmon 1996: 91); that this is value added rather than time taken away from studies (Edwards and Hammond 1998).

Most commentators relate the problems inherent in promoting discussion via an online system when the normal cues that inform and enrich face to face discussion are missing. Edwards and Hammond (1998: 322) refer to 'reticence in joining a public debate particularly when [their] contribution was permanent and there for all to scrutinise'. Responses from our students suggested that they too found this a factor: 'What I don't like is the semi-permanence of the thing. Having posted something, I then wish I could go back and rub it out.'

Equally, the very process of committing thoughts to the forum can leave some students feeling vulnerable and at risk. The permanence of the medium, lack of spontaneity and immediacy (Light and Light 1999) and the 'simultaneous act of typing and thinking' (Grint 1992: 163) can all inhibit participation:

> Can it really be a discussion without a fairly immediate response? It certainly doesn't feel like one. And if the idea is to make a more considered response by working on it offline then I do not find myself motivated to do so as I have more pressing ideas which require consideration.

> In the same way as sending an email – our responses are more measured and rather stilted. However, you can choose whether you would like to reply to a thread which you may not do in a face to face situation.

Some commentators suggest that the 'anonymity' of the medium may encourage those students who do not traditionally take part in group discussions to contribute (Graham *et al.* 1999; Light and Light 1999). This was not a consideration voiced by our students, possibly because of a more mature approach to discussion among postgraduates and the strong links that emerge within groups during the course of their training.

In recognition of the demands already existing on the PGCE course, use of the forum was not mandatory. This had been a factor in the successful (as judged by the students) conduct of asynchronous discussion among distance learning students. There have been suggestions (Hiltz 1997; Graham *et al.* 1999; Jones *et al.* 1999) that an element of compulsion (requirement to participate or even assessment of the amount or nature of participation) may be necessary to encourage active participation and the possibility of building a community of learners. With this in mind students were actively encouraged to access the forum to follow up on issues raised during formal taught sessions on the course. It was also suggested that they posted to the forum issues relating to their course that were of interest to all, such as assignment dates or requirements for planning.

Certainly problems emerge, as here, in attempting to graft a discussion forum on to an existing course structure without allowing participants time and reflection to develop appropriate skills in supporting the discourse. Despite this, transcripts of the discussion and an analysis (in the following section) of how eventually our participating students made sustained use of the forum in response to their interests and needs suggest that they saw it as adding value rather than adding workload.

Building an online community on the PGCE course

As conferences unfold and expand, many participants engage in some active learning, especially through widening their own viewpoints and appreciating differing perspectives.

(Salmon 2000: 32)

The time span of the following supported discussion was relatively short (four months) and effective use was eventually demonstrated by only a restricted number of students, although the aim was to look at the possibility of widening access (in time and space) to continuing discussion in future courses. The students who did participate demonstrated an ability to contribute to a 'community of practice' (however restricted) that openly shared ideas and experiences, while also engaging in lively debate.

PGCE students begin their course with a wide range of personal ICT experiences and attitudes, but generally with little recent experience of ICT in the primary school, and possibly only dim memories of the early BBC computer from their own primary days. Before beginning the course and engagement in the online discussion, the students were asked to reflect on their experiences of, and attitudes to, the use of computers – at home, at work and in education. Their responses highlighted the 'diverse level of skills brought by the students on entry to the course' (Simpson *et al.* 1998: 439). Most of the students wrote in great detail of their experiences and were willing to describe their feelings and even anxieties in the use of ICT. Key issues raised in the responses to the activity were their previous experience in study and the workplace, observations in school and concerns about the effective use of the Internet in the classroom.

Although few of the students reported extensive use of computers during schooling, most had made use of a word processor during their first degree; those who had completed their degrees more recently had also used email and Internet facilities at university. Many of the students had significant workplace experience in the use of ICT, mostly with common commercial applications: word processing, databases, desktop publishing and, in some cases, spreadsheets. Most students wrote extensively about the all-pervasive nature of ICT in the workplace, at home and in education, many remarking enthusiastically on the benefits they believed ICT brought: 'Had I not grown up in a time when computers have existed throughout my working life, I may have had greater opposition to their use.' One student described his reaction to the introduction of computers into his working life (in graphic design): 'My initial reservations soon waned once their appropriateness to design became apparent ... Elements of work became less tedious. Some of the more mundane tasks were eliminated completely.'

There were, however, indications that feelings of competence with the new technology had not always been easily gained:

My early experiences of computers led to unnecessary fear and avoidance through my own ignorance. This eventually paved the way to frustration when I realized what I had missed out on and how useful it would be to have those skills for the future.

I have not been discouraged by my experience with computers. Rather, it has made me all the more determined to learn, because I have now seen how exciting, not to mention how useful, they can be.

In preparation for their PGCE year the students spend a full week in the primary school before joining the course. During this week, few students experienced the use of ICT, either integrated across the curriculum or used in support of children's learning. This was mostly attributed to the early point in the school year during which this experience occurred. However, when asked in the discussion forum to reflect their impression of the contribution of ICT to learning in the primary school, most could discuss perceived benefits, listing collaboration, exploration, opportunities to individualize work, motivation and the raising of self esteem (particularly in a special educational needs context). Many raised pertinent issues and concerns such as the need to still acquire 'basic' skills of handwriting and spelling. They also expressed concerns that much of the ICT they had actually witnessed had been 'copying up' best work and use of the computer for distraction or as a reward for good behaviour. These observations reflected current concerns about limited practice in ICT and demonstrated an ability to comment critically upon the nature of ICT in the classroom even before they had started their course. However, some also experienced examples of good practice and were able to reflect on what they had seen: 'One of the first things I noticed when the children had time on the computer was that they were not afraid of the machine or to make mistakes ... Most of the early lessons were given over to the "trial and error" method of learning. Why? Is it because they have no fear of failure and therefore they can take risks?'

There were concerns expressed about the use of the Internet in the classroom, many echoing common apprehensions about the amount of information available, the problems of helping children to identify and search effectively for information and the possibility of access to 'inappropriate' material: 'Because the information is usually presented so well with colourful pictures, they have a tendency to just copy what is there rather than to digest the information and present it in their own way. It is not always clear whether they are learning anything.'

They also began to identify some of the management issues associated with integrating ICT across the curriculum and the implications for teachers' own knowledge and understanding of the use of ICT. Overall the impression gained from these reflections was that the group had varying experience with ICT but almost all were eager to extend their own competence and looking forward to learning about the role of ICT in the primary school: 'My knowledge and confidence in computing has definitely improved over the years, although I know there is a lot of room for development. I find the idea of teaching ICT quite daunting and maybe my time in schools will be a two-way learning experience. My aim will be to gain more confidence in my own skills and learn about the different ways that new computer and communication technology can be used in schools.'

Following a first flurry of postings, when over 100 contributions were made in response to the first taught session, the forum went quiet apart from some general course enquiries answered by tutors and requests for help with technical matters that were by this point answered most often student to student. The second ICT session, accessed online from the forum site and with a requirement to respond back to the forum, once again produced some thoughtful contributions in response to a posting from the tutor but with little student to student interaction.

At this stage it appeared that the forum offered no benefit in the eyes of the majority of students, while they were still campus-based and heavily timetabled. A posting from a student ICT specialist at the end of September, however, changed the nature of interactions in the forum and established a small group of persistent users. The posting titled 'Do primary pupils need computers' read: 'Thought the article below (from *TES* online) might provoke some stimulating thoughts over the weekend . . .' and attached a article from *TES* online reporting on the views of an American organization, the 'Alliance for Childhood', on the 'obsession with computers in primary schools' (Davies 2000). Reaction in the forum was swift and passionate with strong opinions, and online identities emerging among the dozen students who responded:

There are some valid points . . . It is easy to be swept up in the ICT euphoria without stopping to think . . . The use of computers [described in the article] in most cases was irrelevant and used as a tag-on . . . it goes back to the overall idea that if it ain't no good (i.e. enhances, broadens or adds to the learning objective) don't use it!

. . . found myself wondering if the current eagerness to harness the world wide web wasn't a touch of running before we could walk (or read or write). I'm still of the mind though that it has some benefit but am struggling to work out where and at the expense of what!

One good argument for introducing children to computers in the primary school is that it does to some extent level out the social effect . . .

I am of the opinion that the educational efficacy of ICT in the primary school has been much overstated . . . It was great to have an 'authoritative' source echoing my thoughts . . . I get the impression that this is a minority view at the moment. However, your point about advantaged children having stolen a march on disadvantaged children by Year 7 is one that needs to be addressed. I have discussed this with teachers, in relation to private French lessons at Year 6, who insist that within a year they simply catch up.

I find your idea very interesting – I think it would be worth researching to see whether children who have positive experiences of using ICT in the primary school do go on to have an advantage in secondary – and perhaps more interesting would be to see how this affects their approach to other subjects (is there any research already?)

I do think that ICT is different in that it affects every subject, and can be used to approach subjects in very different ways. I found the article interesting and provocative, and there are some good points – I think that there are lots of examples of ICT being used inappropriately (there is a section at the *TES* website dedicated to ICT disasters). But I do feel that the article confuses the ways in which ICT is being used with ICT as a whole. I think the key factor is how ICT is used in the classroom; whether it is used to enhance learning, or whether it is just being used for the sake of it.

This final comment came once again from one of the ICT specialists along with a request to establish a separate discussion area for each subject specialism which could be used to exchange resources and share common experiences. The idea quickly caught on and soon activity within each separate forum was centred on the exchange of web addresses, attachments downloaded from the Internet and the exchange of ideas for planning for subject activities in school.

A week later a spontaneous posting, from someone who had previously admitted to lurking on the forum, reopened the debate. The posting sparked a lively exchange of views late one Tuesday evening between two students from different study groups:

> . . . interesting interview on Radio 4 about computers in schools . . . about an LEA [local education authority] that aims to get ahead of the government targets for computers in schools. They are aiming to get each child their own laptop with a combination of commercial financing and parental contributions . . . means tested parental contributions of up to £5 a week . . . those who cannot pay will be allowed computers but not to take home. They want to move from learning to use computers to using computers to learn. They quoted a report that schools with good IT [information technology] get good results. But is it the other way round? Are other areas of education suffering as a result of all the IT money?

A response came quickly from one of the forum enthusiasts:

> I can appreciate the sentiment of wanting every child to have their own computer and using this as the basis for learning. I would however be worried that other areas of the curriculum such as handwriting, spelling, practical art and music may be neglected. There are areas which would definitely benefit from permanent access to a computer such as investigative science and maths. But when it comes to music and art nothing can replace actual physical contact with, and experimenting with, the elements involved. Similarly, although communication is taking on more and more advanced forms, I can't imagine a world where writing by hand becomes completely redundant.

At this point a tutor comment asked about the contribution of digital art and within ten minutes the student was back online to defend her position:

> . . . however, handwriting can often prevent children from expressing themselves as freely as they would wish. Computers can free them from the issues of producing clear, legible, correctly spelt work and enable them to concentrate on creativity. In music and art the computer can be used to stimulate interest and create ideas. It can also be used to create music and art itself. I don't think it will ever replace the children's desire to splash paint and bang tambourines.

The exchange then prompted another student to refer back to the discussion on the *TES* online article and add a web address for the full text of the original reviewed writing.

In early October the students went back into school for one day a week in preparation for their five-week placement. Those students who had become established now made lively use of the forum to share initial impressions. They also began to make use of each other's expertise rather than directing such queries directly to the tutor:

My school has two or three PCs in every classroom and an Acorn or two dotted here and there. They are all linked to the web . . . There is a definite anti-ICT feel about the place however and I didn't see anything inspiring – am I allowed to be so critical?

. . . have to say my school is well up on ICT – fully functional suite plus PCs in the classroom, all networked together and on the Internet.

My school had one PC in the classroom with Word on it but not much else . . . any ideas from the ICT specialists on what I can do with very limited technology?

The evolving discussion then centred on the provision of ICT resources in allocated schools. In particular, issues related to different models of resourcing, one or two PCs in the classroom or a separate networked suite, provoked a consideration of how such provision might dictate an approach to planning and management of activities:

Each classroom only has one PC . . . it makes it almost impossible for them to be used effectively, simply because it would take ages for all the children to have a go, by which time the impetus would be lost.

. . . the computers are arranged in groups of four in resource areas between the classroom. This enables 4 groups of children to work at a time. . . . Even if a school has relatively few computers, by arranging them together, classes can book times to use them.

The need to plan for the forthcoming placement once again caused a rush of activity on the forum. Ease with the system, a need to communicate and an easy familiarity among participants made this a fruitful exercise with examples of collaboration and sharing of practice. Much of this discussion, including the two-way exchange below, sits comfortably within the fourth stage of Salmon's model.

. . . just found out what unit of work is planned for my children next half term. It's a multimedia presentation, mixed Y5/6 class, they are timetabled for 15 minutes whole-class teaching and half an hour per child per week. I haven't found any interesting software in school. I'm not even sure what a multimedia presentation is and feel the panic rising!

Hi, I too have to teach multimedia and am trying to think of good ideas. Perhaps we could help each other out?

Great . . . found out more today. The children have been downloading images from World War II and the teacher had an idea of putting them into a PowerPoint presentation. Does this count as multimedia?

Eventually the first student posted a long message on the forum. Her writing is almost private musing, as if the act of writing is helping her to organize her thoughts. It is gratifying that she chose to do this in a public forum:

> . . . having sat down to plan my first ICT input I'm panicking again. I had planned to do multimedia authoring using PowerPoint. For the first session I intended to have two things for the children – a worksheet based on Vivi Lachs' CD-ROM (Lachs 2000) to inspire them to the possibilities and then a worksheet based on PowerPoint to familiarize themselves with the software. There are several problems with this!
>
> (1) I have never used PowerPoint before and although I am trying to familiarize myself with it as fast as possible I don't know if it can actually do the non-linear stuff as per Vivi's CD (so do I want to inspire them to something they won't be able to create?). (2) I have discovered how difficult it is to create a worksheet when totally unfamiliar with the software. I really don't think I have the skill to do this from scratch. (3) Seeing how complex the software is and how endless the possibilities I wonder if the project as I have designed it is too ambitious for the children in the timeframe.
>
> I am now wondering whether to do something much more structured. I found a book in the Curriculum Centre [at the University] today which was a scheme of work for introducing PowerPoint software. While this didn't look particularly inspiring it would at least give me the scaffolding I need for familiarizing myself with the software and I could adapt it to fit in with my project as I go along. I am of course concerned that if I abandon my plan at the first hurdle I will not be able to complete my assignment satisfactorily – but if I do need to change tack it seems to make sense to do this now before I am in any deeper. Can you offer some suggestions for ways forward please!

Good news I went to the secondary school today with Y6 so they could spend the morning using PowerPoint. Have now got a clearer picture of what we can do. Do you want to meet and talk about this?

Two days later the student again posted to the forum:

Having spent the weekend thinking (and having some useful input from K, – thanks) I have decided to alter my plan as follows. Spend the initial sessions working through my teacher's plans for the topic which means that the children will be putting text with their images. Next we will get the class to structure their work. While they are doing this I can be familiarizing myself more with the software. When they have decided how they want to put their work together I can then introduce them to the particular bits of the software they need, rather than trying to get them to play with the whole lot. Does this seem a more sensible plan?

At the beginning of November the students went into school full-time. Activity in the forum now took on a more social aspect, with students keen to swap experiences but also to keep in touch from widely spread schools. The forum provided an opportunity for the students to 'transcend [the teacher's] traditional isolation within classrooms' (Dawes 2001: 70) and gain support from their peers.

Conclusion

There is much claimed for the use of CMC within the wider world of education, and correspondingly many examples of discussions that have foundered, leaving tutors frustrated and students disillusioned. In truth, the tutor effort needed to foster use of this forum was substantial: nearly 50 per cent of the postings and a commitment to access at least once a day, including weekends! However, what has emerged is the recognition that the facility offered a unique opportunity to extend tutor/student and student/student interaction beyond the restrictions of time and place. Once familiar and comfortable with the system the students displayed many of the attributes suggested by Edwards and Hammond (1998) as crucial in sustaining critical engagement in the learning community. They were willing to share an incomplete but developing understanding and trusted each other sufficiently to risk misinterpretation and disagreement.

References

Davies, D. (2000) Another voice: do primary pupils need computers? *TES* online, http://www.tes.co.uk (accessed 14 Nov. 2001).

Dawes, L. (2001) What stops teachers using new technology?, in A. Loveless and E. Ellis (eds) *ICT, Pedagogy and the Curriculum*. London: Routledge Falmer.

DfEE (Department for Education and Employment) (1998) *Teaching: High Status, High Standards*, Circular no. 4198 (*Requirements for Courses of Initial Teacher Training*). London: DfEE.

Edwards, E. and Hammond, M. (1998) Introducing e-mail into a distance learning course – a case study, *Innovations in Education and Training International*, 35(4).

Graham, M., Scarborough, H. and Goodwin, C. (1999) Implementing computer mediated communication in an undergraduate course – a practical experience, *Journal of Asynchronous Learning Networks*, 3(1), see http://www.aln.org/alnweb/journal/jaln-vol3issue1.htm (accessed 14 Nov. 2001).

Grint, K. (1992) Sniffers, lurkers, actor networkers: computer mediated communications as a technical fix, in J. Beynon and H. McKay (eds) *Technical Literacy and the Curriculum*. London: Falmer.

Hiltz, S.R. (1997) Impacts of college level courses via asynchronous learning networks: some preliminary results, *Journal of Asynchronous Learning Networks*, 1(2), see http://www.aln.org/alnweb/journal/jaln-vol1issue2.htm (accessed 14 Nov. 2001).

Jones, C., Asensio, M. and Goodyear, P. (1999) Networked learning in higher education. Paper given at the ALT-C99 Conference, Bristol.

Kolb, D. (1984) *Experiential Learning: Experience as the Source of Learning and Development*. Englewood Cliffs, NJ: Prentice Hall.

Lachs, V. (2000) *Making Multimedia in the Classroom*. London: Routledge Falmer.

Laurillard, D. (1993) *Rethinking University Teaching*. London: Routledge.

Leask, M. (ed.) (2001) *Issues in Teaching Using ICT*. London: Routledge Falmer.

Light, P. and Light, V. (1999) Analysing asynchronous learning interactions: computer-mediated communication in a conventional undergraduate setting, in K. Littleton and P. Knight (eds) *Learning with Computers: Analysing Productive Interaction*. London: Routledge.

Loveless, A., DeVoogd, G. and Bohlin, R. (2001) Something old, something new: is pedagogy affected by ICT?, in A. Loveless and V. Ellis (eds) *ICT, Pedagogy and the Curriculum*. London: Routledge Falmer.

McLoughlin, C. and Oliver, R. (1999) Pedagogic roles and dynamics in telematics environments, in M. Selinger and J. Pearson (eds) *Telematics in Education: Trends and Issues*. Oxford: Elsevier.

Nixon, T. and Salmon, G. (1996) Computer-mediated learning and its potential, in R. Mills and A. Tait (eds) *Supporting the Learner in Open and Distance Learning*. London: Pitman.

Salmon, G. (2000) *E-Moderating: The Key to Teaching and Learning Online*. London: Kogan Page.

Selinger, M. and Pearson, J. (1999) *Telematics in Education: Trends and Issues*. Oxford: Elsevier.

Simpson, M., Payne, F., Munro, R. and Lynch, E. (1998) Using Information and communications technology as a pedagogical tool, *Journal of Information Technology in Teacher Education*, 7(3): 430–46.

Stratfold, M. (1999) Promoting learner dialogues on the web, in M. Eisenstadt and T. Vincent (eds) *The Knowledge Web: Learning and Collaborating on the Net*. London: Kogan Page.

10

POTENTIAL INTO PRACTICE: DEVELOPING ICT IN THE PRIMARY CLASSROOM

Martin Torjussen and Elizabeth Coppard

In this final chapter, two teachers discuss how they developed their practice in using information and communication technology (ICT) in the primary classroom as they began their professional development during a PGCE course. As beginning teachers, they outline the processes involved in planning, preparing, implementing and evaluating the use of ICT to support children's learning in art. They address the change in roles and relationships between teacher and children as definitions of 'expert' and 'novice' with ICT are challenged and exploratory ways of working are encouraged. They also discuss the issues of evaluating and assessing the children's achievements and needs.

A rationale for using ICT in art with young children

Elizabeth Coppard presents a rationale for using ICT in art and design in the primary school, based upon her first teaching experiences in a primary classroom.

In art and design the computer can be seen as just another tool to be used in the same way as any other media, contributing towards 'the broad field of experience which we should be offering children' (Mathieson 1993: 17). All tools, including computers, have their advantages and disadvantages, making them appropriate for different purposes. Can the use of ICT offer anything, other than what is already available through the use of traditional media, to support learning in art and design? There have been many claims that ICT can provide the sort of engaging environment that is ideal for learning, resulting in the development of higher-level thinking skills and the extension of physical abilities. This rationale explores these claims and the implications for teachers that arise from them.

One of the main features of a computer that can assist learning is its interactive nature. Interactive methods of learning are more likely to motivate and interest pupils. Mathieson found that when the computer was used for purposeful tasks, it triggered children's 'natural curiosity', 'willingness to learn' and 'desire to investigate' (1993: 18–19). He found that this enabled children to work more intensely for longer periods of time.

I found that the children I taught were generally enthusiastic about art and design. Using the computer certainly generated excitement and some pupils who seemed reluctant to participate in other art activities were more motivated. The interactive nature of the computer promotes active, experimental learning. It allows pupils to try out different possibilities, see the consequences of decisions and actions, and plan the next move accordingly.

Experimental learning is also promoted by the computer's provisionality. Work can be revised easily on graphic software, unlike traditional media such as charcoal or paint. This allows children to develop their ideas by evaluating and revising their work. Images can be moved, repeated or enlarged and colours can be substituted easily, allowing children to investigate the effects of these changes. This type of work is likely to increase children's understanding of the techniques and language of art and design. For many children who lack confidence in their drawing ability, the provisionality of the computer makes it a non-threatening environment for learning. Most children in the class in which I worked were able to progress beyond the initial set task through interaction with each other. They worked in groups of mixed artistic and ICT capabilities and were very curious to know how their peers achieved certain effects, as they wanted to be able to produce them too. The skills needed were quickly transferred through conversation and demonstration, so that before long the whole group was experimenting with similar techniques. ICT provided a good social context for learning by encouraging children to collaborate.

Although computers can assist learning, it is important to remember that there are also times when using the computer can get in the way of learning or suppress creativity. A few children who were initially excited about using the computer became frustrated as they found their difficulties in controlling the mouse limited what they were able to produce. When evaluating their work most of the children who showed a high level of enthusiasm for art and design said that they preferred using traditional materials to the computer. The reasons the children gave included lack of control and a limited range of colours and effects in comparison to using paint or collage.

One of the main issues for teachers using ICT is the way in which they view the role of the computer in the classroom, as this will have an impact on how effectively it is used in their teaching. Some teachers see ICT as a tutor and assume that children will be taught *by* it. Although ICT does have characteristics that can support and extend learning, children working with computers will not automatically learn better. In order to produce good quality computer art, children need to learn ICT skills and combine these with their artistic skills to select elements to create a cohesive piece. Children could not achieve this without clear direction from the teacher. The role of the teacher is vital in providing appropriate structure, direction and guidance in children's learning. Teachers must decide when and when not to use computers. When they do use ICT they need to make sure it is used for challenging, purposeful, integrated tasks.

Many teachers see ICT as a neutral tool. They are likely to use the computer to complete tasks that could have been done using other methods, mainly for presentation, or as an extra rather than an integrated part of the lesson. Teachers need to understand the educational potential of ICT so that they can integrate it effectively and get the most out of it. The computer is a cognitive tool that can be used to enhance children's learning by allowing them to do things only possible with a computer, such as manipulating images. If teachers are to be able to teach effectively they must have a basic technical capability as this will enable them to approach ICT with the confidence and competence needed to create as many effective learning opportunities as possible. Another issue that arises for teachers is the evaluation of artwork carried out on the computer. Although the criteria for assessing computer art are the same as those for assessing art in any other medium, the use of ICT can confuse the issue. Automatic functions can improve presentation without improving the artistic content of a piece. Teachers must be able to distinguish between a pupil's progress in the subject area and in the development of their ICT capability.

It is clear that the use of ICT can support learning in art and design by providing an interactive, motivating and safe environment that encourages experimentation. ICT can also extend learning in art and design by providing unique facilities that allow work to be revised, manipulated and transferred from one medium to another. However, this is dependent on the ability of the teacher to use ICT appropriately in an integrated and purposeful way. It is essential that new teachers are aware of the educational potential of ICT and that they maintain a positive but critical attitude towards it so that it is used appropriately.

Planning, preparing and evaluating art activities with ICT

Martin Torjussen worked with a Year 2 class (6- and 7-year-olds) at a primary school near the centre of Brighton. The school had recently been equipped with a new computer suite of ten PCs and a colour printer. He worked on a project linking art and ICT in the curriculum using simple painting software ('Paint' and 'Dazzle'). The stimulus for work in the ICT suite was the paintings of Joan Miró, which the children had studied in their curriculum art sessions. Martin began by introducing the software to the children in the ICT suite and encouraging them to familiarize themselves with its features through free play.

One of my points of interest was to compare children's responses to using both software and traditional painting materials. I also envisaged that this might encourage children to be more critical of the tools that they use in art, and begin to choose between them more appropriately. In developing their own Miró reproductions my expectations were that children would initially achieve better results with pencil/paint/paper because of their familiarity with the medium. I anticipated that they would find the software more exciting to work with but that it would pose more difficulties in achieving the desired output.

ICT and the roles of teacher and child

One of the effects of the emergence of ICT as a dominant player in primary education will surely be, if it has not already happened, a dramatic change in the role of the teacher and their working relationships with the child. While 'virtual schools' are still of the future, even an elementary level of learning on a PC can change the traditional roles of giver and receiver. McKeown states that 'using ICT often makes the relationship between pupil and teacher – the expert up front who is seen as some kind of challenge – less confrontational. The teaching may involve more discussion and less listening; more experimentation and problem solving and less showmanship. Using ICT is not an easy option and involves a risk-taking approach by both staff and learners' (McKeown 1999).

This was certainly the case in lessons where, after I had demonstrated and modelled a few key tools to the children, they were given the opportunity and time to explore the software at their own pace and with, as we shall see later, their own sense of risk. This made my role less intrusive and more consultative. There was no end result to be achieved and as a consequence I was neither enforcer nor informer, neither setting rules nor bringing my own knowledge to bear on the children's work, unless specifically asked to do so.

I did not want to be seen to be doing too much, feeling, as Bennett (1997: 67) observes, that 'teachers often feel torn between showing children what to do and letting them find out for themselves'. While this is obviously the case throughout the curriculum it is even more apparent in an ICT activity where the ability levels of the children may be difficult to judge for the inexperienced teacher. Do they all know to click the left side of the mouse for the majority of tasks? Do they use the right side of the mouse at all/appropriately? Can they move the mouse correctly? Will they remember from the 'play' activity what each tool actually does, and be able to use this later in the more structured sessions? For this reason the children were given as much 'play' time as possible and encouraged to explore new ways of working with the software and to try and remember what each tool could do.

Because of the size of each group (I used groups of six to eight children of mixed ability) I was able to judge quickly the competence levels on display and give extra tuition to those showing signs of discouragement, though again after waiting for a request to be made. Much can be learned on the computer with the attitude 'I wonder what this does?' or 'What will happen if I do this?' *if only* the user has the confidence to try it. This kind of explorative learning helps to assist the roles of teacher and pupil.

The anonymity of a computer provides a safe environment to explore and investigate. Perhaps the reason why children are able to do this is because the computer is a multi-levelled tool, and can be as easy or as difficult as the user makes it. This is certainly true after a certain level of competence has been acquired. Peter Scrimshaw (1997: 105) writes that 'users can choose for themselves the level of complexity of that content, and the level of sophistication of the manipulation of it. This encourages learning, by reducing the risk of frustration and failure'. It is a world in which the permanent is undermined by the temporary and, unless every stage is printed out or saved, mistakes remain relatively private and forays into the unknown are supported by known ways of escaping, deleting or starting again.

However, it must be made clear that ICT hardware and software may be no better or worse than any other resource in the school. It is the way in which they are used by the teacher to aid the child's learning that is important. Making children aware of the diversity of ICT is crucial to their learning, as is encouraging the appropriate application of the resource. There must always be time built in for reflection and analysis of a task after stage completion or final completion. For example, when the Miró reproductions using ICT were displayed on the wall next to their painted counterparts, it was interesting to discuss with the children which method they felt was most successful or most enjoyable, and the various merits and demerits of the two forms. As Sanger *et al.* (1997: 173) write of their research findings into experiences of new technologies, 'The very lack of children's work and conversation concerning their experiences of work-based technologies, whilst at school, spoke volumes for the way that schools could create a taboo about children's activity'.

It was beneficial to all children to review each other's work after certain stages of the task. Those who found the task challenging could learn techniques used by their peers to achieve certain visual effects. They might come to economize on their labour through picking up shortcuts – learning that the right click on the mouse is a quicker way to use the cut/copy/paste tools than through the menu toolbar, or that using Ctrl X/C/V is even more effective. The children who had accomplished most were encouraged to articulate their own strategies, which not only taught these skills to others but cemented them in their own minds, and made their learning more tangible and rewarding. It is through using this type of forum of discussion and appraisal of activity that children come to understand the nature of ICT and how it affects their work. They will become more selective in their use of tools and less dependent on one way of learning.

Planning for teaching and learning

There were several learning intentions underpinning the activities using ICT to reproduce Miró's work. The focus for the first was that the children should familiarize themselves with the software '*Paint*' and '*Dazzle*' through free play. The idea of free play was crucial to their understanding, not only of the software but also of the way that much is learned in an ICT environment: that is, through experimentation, exploration and 'safe' decision making. Time spent here would profit their interaction with the resources in future lessons. The second learning intention was art-orientated: to reproduce a Miró painting using different media. As this series of lessons ran parallel to the children attempting to reproduce the same painting using paper and paint, it was possible to set up the project as a direct comparison between 'traditional' and 'new' methods of art. Within this investigation fell another learning intention: to understand that colour, positioning, size of related parts and shape may vary from painting to screen. This ensured a consideration of mathematical names for common two-dimensional shapes, of sorting shapes and describing their features, of making patterns using shapes, of recognizing symmetry and of using mathematical vocabulary to describe position, direction and movement. The articulation demanded by this area attempted to enhance the child's listening and speaking skills, in particular through questioning and expanding vocabulary. The final learning intentions were explicitly ICT-orientated: to save, reload and print; to improve and hone fine motor skills through mouse/keyboard control.

The activities

To start with the children were introduced to the paintings of the Spanish artist Joan Miró. They were given a short biographical outline of Miró's life, and time was spent expressing likes and dislikes of his paintings, using poster reproductions. It was made clear that the paintings the pupils were seeing were reproductions. This helped to introduce the idea of art reproduction, and also paved the way for questions about the differences in size or tone that were to become apparent in their work later. For instance, as the posters did not represent the true size of the paintings, some children were spaced out in a rectangle to show how the size of the posters was often misleading. As their own later images would be much smaller even than the posters, this was helpful in introducing the subject of dimensions. Some postcard reproductions were also shown, as this not only confirmed what had been discussed concerning size, but also showed some subtle colour differences, suggesting that reproductions are not always faithful to their originals. This was used later to support those who felt that they could not achieve a 'true' depiction of a given painting.

The first major activity in terms of achieving a final product was in producing a Miró painting using paint and paper. Children were encouraged to experiment with different paints, to see which suited their purpose best, and to explore mixing, colouring, shape and space within a 'traditional' art lesson format. The activities that followed occurred within the ICT suite. Children were encouraged to reproduce Miró paintings using the now familiar software. Time was spent teaching skills such as saving, opening and printing files, and the children were able to choose manipulation of tools to suit their own taste.

Organization

While the introduction and the art lesson were whole-class activities, the ICT-based tasks were undertaken in mixed ability groups of between six and eight pupils. I was fortunate to be able to take groups into the ICT suite, leaving the remainder of the class to work with a teaching assistant. Each group was timetabled for half an hour a week, but there was some scope within the timetable for possible supplementary time – Friday afternoons, for example. The task was initially discussed as a whole group, with clear objectives given to the children. This was also the time to remind the children of expectations of their behaviour in the suite, with the health and safety implications made clear. The children were reminded of the skills and techniques they had used in their free play sessions, and encouraged to recall what they had learned during this time. After this I modelled part of a Miró painting on screen, and children were called upon to suggest how I had achieved certain effects, and also to identify which Miró painting I was attempting to reproduce. This initial review and modelling session lasted no more than eight to ten minutes.

Following this, the groups were each given 'play' time on their computer to achieve some part of a Miró painting reproduction. They were able to select their own painting, and to 'paint' whichever part they chose. This allowed them to select according to their own confidence and ability. This differentiation by choice was crucial to their own sense of independence in their learning. Most chose, if not straight away then certainly by the end of the first session, to attempt achievable tasks, ones which they knew they had the skills and knowledge of the tools to fulfil. At several stages during this session the children were stopped and asked to articulate their learning. Some were asked how they achieved a particular shape or colour, some were asked about their preferred methods of software painting. They were also asked to recall how certain tasks such as saving/reloading and printing could be done, in order to confirm their own understanding and remind their classmates who may have been struggling. There were also opportunities given, to those children who felt that they could, to show the group a new technique learned.

Throughout the activity children were selected to help their classmates who had asked me for help. In passing this role over to the children, we instituted a peer tutoring system whereby the more experienced could extend their understanding of the task and articulate their skills to those less experienced. It was important that each child was given the opportunity to demonstrate skills to the other children, at whatever level, as this helped both group dynamics and reinforced learning for those who needed it. As each group progressed, they were called upon to produce more and more of their chosen painting. In the fourth week they were primarily concerned with the final product. All children were required to have a 'final print' after which nothing could be altered – this helped to develop their understanding of progression and final outcome.

Evaluation of the children's work took place as a whole class. We considered what our initial objectives had been, and whether or not we had achieved them. We discussed how we had progressed throughout the four-week period, and what we had learned. We looked at the final products, and compared them critically to the Miró reproductions. Differences between the children's paintings were highlighted to show the different ways certain visual effects had been accomplished. Techniques were articulated and evaluated by all the children. Preferences were given, but not in terms of right/wrong solutions: each child had been encouraged to select their own way of learning. Finally the computer images were compared to the art lesson final products. Preferences were stated between the two in terms of manipulation and output. Both forms were displayed in the classroom side by side.

Assessment of individual, finished work

For the beginning teacher, initial assessment in ICT is sometimes difficult to judge. Whereas assessment of a child's literacy, numeracy or science knowledge can often be drawn from the child's workbooks, it is less easy to know whether a child is comfortable and confident in front of a computer. Finished ICT work can be ambiguous in terms of assessment; it is not always clear what was achieved during the task. This is evident for the teacher once the class has begun – how do you assess ability levels when tasks can be so multifarious and outcomes so intangible? How do you distinguish between competence, skill and technique, and the ability to engage in the higher-order processes of 'exchanging and sharing information' or 'developing ideas' (DfEE/QCA 2000).

Analysis of finished work from our project might raise some of the following questions: Does a child who does not select the 'circle' tool to draw Miró's moon do so from ignorance or preference? Does the child who selects the 'spraycan' tool to 'fill' an object do so knowing that the 'paint-can' tool does this much quicker? Has the child been able to open/save/ print their work? Have they been able to modify an image once drawn, or have they been satisfied with the size and position of the first attempt?

Conclusions

There are some observers who suggest that the challenges posed by ICT tools are greater than those set by traditional methods. According to Bennett (1997: 53), 'the advantage of a drawing package is the flexibility it provides in editing pictures. The disadvantage is that they can be fiddly for young children to use'. This implies that children would find using these tools harder than re-creating Miró's paintings with a paint-brush and paint, something that was discussed in the final class analysis of the display. While conceding that some children found using a mouse difficult, initially at least, and that within a drawing package some tools require the utmost control, I did not find that they were 'fiddly' for the children. No more so than a pencil, rubber, ruler, shoelace, coins, small toys or any other thing that requires dexterity and a controlled applica-tion of fine motor skills. Interestingly, the class was split more or less evenly between the most effective way of reproducing a painting. Andrew said that the computer was 'easy'; Megan agreed but stated that she didn't like 'normal painting' anyway. Harry said that he liked to use the computer 'for other things' and that with 'painting you can draw and paint really big things'. Rachel liked the peer tutoring, 'showing them what you can do' while Shannon said that sometimes she wanted to work it out for herself. Out of 33 children, 20 thought that the paintings on the computer were 'better' than those created with paint.

Drawing packages are there to be mastered, like any other software, and a lack of consistency between the painting to be copied and the children's final reproduction might be down to a number of limited skills: perception and perspective for example. And, as has already been mentioned, the software matches the task to the abilities of the child; there is no criterion by which the child shall be judged other than from where they started. Accordingly I was happier with those from a low starting base who applied themselves and produced something that they were satisfied with, than with those whose reproductions were skilled but whose initial skill level promised more. Throughout the project the emphasis was on the role of free play to further learning in ICT. This in turn led to changes in the roles of teacher and children to the extent that, at one stage, the children implemented the peer tutoring system to such effect that my presence in the ICT suite was almost superfluous.

References

Bennett, R. (1997) *Teaching IT*. Oxford: Nash Pollock Publishing.

DfEE/QCA (Department for Education and Employment/Qualifications and Curriculum Authority) (2000) *The National Curriculum: Handbook for Primary Teachers in England*. London: DfEE/QCA.

Mathieson, K. (1993) *Children's Art and the Computer*. Sevenoaks: Hodder & Stoughton.

McKeown, S. (1999) Stay cool, log on, *Guardian Education Online*, http://www.guardian.co.uk/ (accessed 11 May 1999).

Sanger, J., Willson, J., Davies, B. and Whitakker, R. (1997) *Young Children, Videos and Computer Games: Issues for Teachers and Parents*. London: Falmer.

Scrimshaw, P. (1997) Computers and the teacher's role, in B. Somekh and N. Davis (eds) *Using Information Technology Effectively in Teaching and Learning*. London: Routledge.

INDEX

Page references in italics indicate diagrams, tables and pictures.